Splendid Encounters

Memoirs of Collaborations, Interactions, and
Conversations with Many of the Most Celebrated
Musicians of the Twentieth Century

by

ABRAHAM KAPLAN
with Dafna (Kaplan) Zilafro
Special Assistance from Dr. Linda Gingrich

iUniverse, Inc.
New York   Bloomington

Splendid Encounters
Memoirs of Collaborations, Interactions, and Conversations with Many of the Most Celebrated Musicians of the Twentieth Century

iUniverse books may be ordered through booksellers or by contacting:

iUniverse
1663 Liberty Drive
Bloomington, IN 47403
www.iuniverse.com
1-800-Authors (1-800-288-4677)

ISBN: 978-1-4401-3199-8 (pbk)
ISBN: 978-1-4401-3200-1 (cloth)
ISBN: 978-1-4401-3201-8 (ebk)

Printed in the United States of America

iUniverse rev. date: 5/1/09

Splendid Encounters

Memoirs of Collaborations, Interactions, and Conversations with Many of the Most Celebrated Musicians of the Twentieth Century

by

ABRAHAM KAPLAN
with Dafna (Kaplan) Zilafro
Special Assistance from Dr. Linda Gingrich

iUniverse, Inc.
New York   Bloomington

Splendid Encounters
Memoirs of Collaborations, Interactions, and Conversations with
Many of the Most Celebrated Musicians of the Twentieth Century

iUniverse books may be ordered through booksellers or by contacting:

iUniverse
1663 Liberty Drive
Bloomington, IN 47403
www.iuniverse.com
1-800-Authors (1-800-288-4677)

ISBN: 978-1-4401-3199-8 (pbk)
ISBN: 978-1-4401-3200-1 (cloth)
ISBN: 978-1-4401-3201-8 (ebk)

Printed in the United States of America

iUniverse rev. date: 5/1/09

My thanks and gratitude go first and foremost to the person most instrumental in making this book a reality, my daughter, Dafna K. Zilafro. Without her persistence, perseverance, and dedication this book would have never seen the light of day. Special thanks to Dr. Linda Gingrich, a former student and colleague who helped with the Addendum chapter, and who provided invaluable editorial suggestions on the entire draft. To my lifelong friend, Robert Markel, for his helpful suggestions concerning the publication of this book. And last but not least, to all of my students at the Juilliard School of Music in New York City (1961-1977), and at the University of Washington in Seattle (1977-2004), who inspired me to draw upon the stories within this book time and again as teaching tools. Special thanks to Samantha Hale and the entire staff of iUniverse for their help in the preparation of the manuscript for publication.

A.K.

CONTENTS

PREFACE

By Dafna [Kaplan] Zilafro

Throughout his forty-plus years as one of the greatest musical teachers of all time, my father has used the following stories to transport his hearers—mostly students of classical music—into another realm, where they might glean jewels of musical wisdom from the great Maestros. It has been my great privilege over the years to interview my father, to record each of these inspirational memories, and to cherish the words, subtle intonations, and passion that he communicates with each anecdote.

My aim was simply to capture my father's magical storytelling faculties in writing, without losing an ounce of the character, intensity, passion, and joy that he exudes in the telling. Although in his forty-plus years as a teacher, *many* have had the benefit of hearing them first hand (some of us more than once, I might add), it is high time that the rest of the world has the same opportunity.

INTRODUCTION

By Abraham Kaplan

As a teacher of music, I have told many of the stories contained in this book because I wanted my students to get the sense that these legendary musicians are real human beings. Perhaps my drive to communicate their humanity evolved out of the following event: When I was studying at the conservatory in Jerusalem, Israel, one of my teachers used to give us assignments to compose music in different styles. We would get to the class, and each of us had to play the composition that we had written on the piano. After one of the classes, a fellow student asked if she could have the pieces that I wrote—I handed her the music, and then forgot about the event. Some time later, on a walk through the conservatory—which was essentially one big auditorium with a number of surrounding classrooms—I saw my fellow student at the piano with an eight-year-old girl, playing a familiar piece. I walked over to them and smiled, realizing that it was my own composition. As I approached, my fellow student turned to the young girl and said, "Tamar, do you know that this man is the composer of what you were just playing?" The little girl looked up at me with two big, beautiful eyes, and said, "Isn't he dead?"

Well, maybe at the time it was funnier—perhaps because I was in my early twenties, with the world by the tail and my whole life in music ahead of me. Now, although I still chuckle, the child's words are profound to me. Many of the great musicians in this book have passed on, and many are getting older, as I am. I have a chance now, like at no other time in history, to revive the living and breathing experiences of a generation that will only be remembered from this point forward in books, television, and publications. I am zealous about telling the stories that fill my life and heart with music. I hope you will enjoy reading even half as much as I've enjoyed retelling and reliving these encounters with giftedness divine.

There's another reason that I wanted to write this book about all of the people who touched my life with their genius and accomplishment. Much to my chagrin most biographies in circulation (Chotzinoff's biography of Toscanini, the two biographies of Bernstein, and the biography of Boulez, for example) are written by non-musicians who seem to be more interested in the gossip about the personal lives of their subjects than the core of these wonderful musicians: their dedication to their art. As a lover of music, I hope to give just a taste of what a fellow music lover might have longed to experience—what a fellow fan might appreciate knowing, hearing, and seeing from the "other side."

What I hope to convey are the emotions associated with each experience, and to share the joys, curiosities, and inspirations that have struck me in my working relationships with the legends of our age.

– 1 –

WILLIAM SCHUMAN

If I could describe Schuman in a phrase, I would say that he was the quintessential American composer—and he would have liked to be described as such.

I met him when I came to Juilliard as a student. I took the Juilliard entrance exam in theory and conducting after graduating from the Israeli Conservatory in Jerusalem. The people who examined me in theory said, "Well, we could pass you to the graduate school, but you know our president, William Schuman, has instituted a new undergraduate program in theory that is different from other conservatory programs. We call it "L & M: Literature & Materials of Music." Now of course, you have already learned in the traditional way, but would you be interested (they noticed that I loved theory) in taking the last year of undergraduate before you move on to graduate school?" I said I would love to, as I was interested in learning a new way. So I went to a class taught by Peter Mennin (who later became the President of Juilliard). The students in the class had already studied theory at other conservatories or with other traditional Juilliard teachers. Mennin wanted to do a survey to find out what everyone knew, so he asked all sorts of specific questions, like "what is a Neapolitan sixth chord?" A few people raised their hands and started philosophizing about their answers. He had a suspicion that they probably didn't know what chord

1

he was asking about. So he asked, "Can anyone spell' the Neapolitan sixth chord in C major?" Up until then I hadn't said anything. Of all these people, nobody raised his or her hand. So I went ahead and spelled it. A few other incidents transpired like this, where students knew the general idea, but the hard facts were not understood. So a few weeks into this class, I noticed that there seemed to be holes in most of the students' education.

Schuman had a wonderful ritual as president. After a few months into every year, he would meet with all of the new students that year, and listen to their questions and comments personally. Very often those who came from other countries had wonderful talents and perspectives to share, but were intimidated when they encountered the richness and breadth of talents possessed by their fellow students. Schuman wanted to know how all of the students were doing. So in the gathering that I witnessed, students kept raising their hands, saying, "Mr. Schuman, maybe I wasn't prepared enough for the L & M class—I am having a hard time"

He explained that he started this course because he himself studied under the old system, where you studied harmony separately, form separately, and counterpoint separately. As a musician, he found it very dry and boring. He thought that if a good teacher would incorporate all of those subjects into one class, it would be much more interesting. Still, the comments came. So I, who was doing very well in L & M level four, thought that I should speak up. I raised my hand and mentioned that I studied the traditional way, doing each one separately studying under specialists in each. I never did find it boring, perhaps because I enjoyed theory. However, after a bit of the L & M class, I discovered that there was a slight problem with the method. For instance, we know that Schubert at the end of his life needed to study more counterpoint.

---

* To a musician, spelling a chord means naming the notes in the chord.

But the teachers that were teaching L & M might be like Schubert. Although they might be good at two of the disciplines, they might not be strong in the third. For this reason I suggested that the three be taught separately, each by a specialist in his or her field. While this might be boring for some, it might also provide the best education. For example, I understand that grammar is boring to study, but it wouldn't hurt a poet to study grammar.

What I found fascinating and wonderful was that I was a new student, barely could express myself in English, but within two years of hearing my input, Schuman modified the L & M Program, first starting with traditional theory (the least boring textbooks that he could find), and then in the last year or two moving students into L & M, where they incorporated those different theories into different pieces of music.

My next encounter with Schuman was when I graduated from Juilliard and decided that it was time to go back to Israel. He had seen me conduct and was trying to talk me into staying in the country. His choral teacher was going to be moving on in about two years, and he wanted to appoint me for the job as head of choral music at Julliard. As a young student, with my Israeli chutzpah intact, I said that I just didn't believe in "waiting around" for a job. I said that I had come from Israel to study, and that I should probably go back. He offered to find me a two-year, temporary professorial job somewhere in the country before coming, and the salary at the time sounded like a dream. In 1958, the beginning salary was $10,000. Nevertheless, I declined and decided to return to Israel.

After a year in Israel, I came back to America with a touring choir. This time, Schuman put his hand on my shoulder and said, "You are not going back! You are starting next season part-time, and then will switch to the head of the choral department."

I had learned something from my year back in Israel—metaphorically, that one cannot be in love with two mistresses. You see, I had two ideas somehow fixed in my head. One was that I wanted to be back in my homeland. The other was that I wanted to make music at the highest level that was available to me. By the time Schuman put his hand on my shoulder that day, I had realized that I couldn't do both things. Obviously, I ended up choosing music, and have never looked back.

Years later I performed some world premieres of Schuman's music. I did a concert of choral music at Circle in the Square, a series of contemporary music in downtown Manhattan. I also performed an opera that he wrote based on the poem *Casey at the Bat*, which forced me to learn all of the rules of baseball very quickly—since it was required to understand much of the timing of the different section entrances.

If you look at his entire compositional output, Schuman's music always had a touch of Americana. If I had to assess the character of his music, I would call it visceral and masculine, if there is such a thing— kind of angular. He was a very modest man as far as his music was concerned. When my father came to visit, they hit it off right away. I don't know if it had to do with the fact that he was my father and Schuman felt paternal toward me—but he described to my father about how he ran his life. He said, "I get up around 6:30 in the morning, have a light breakfast. I go to my shed and write music until 10:00, and then I go over to Juilliard and handle those responsibilities for the day." About his writing music, he said, "I don't know how good it is—I just do my best."

One of his first jobs was as a choral conductor in a girls' college, Sarah Lawrence. But he was never a symphonic conductor, and he didn't continue conducting after that point. He always preferred that conductors like myself perform his choral music, and Bernstein his symphonic music.

After Sarah Lawrence, he was asked to be the director of publishing at G. Schirmer, because he was thoroughly organized and a terrific administrator. Juilliard heard that this fabulous American composer was the administrator there, and they asked him to take the job as President of Juilliard. He at the time, although young, gave them conditions. "First thing, I am not showing up at the office until 11:00. Secondly, don't try to give me advice about how to run the school. If you don't like the way I do it, don't renew my contract." That's how he became president, and he could have done it for the rest of his life.

When Juilliard was going to be integrated into the new Lincoln Center development, Schuman attended all of the meetings. The administration noticed again that he had a very organized mind and a talent for management, and so they asked him to be the president of Lincoln Center. Again, he set conditions: "I don't want to be a landlord. I will become president if Lincoln Center will initiate a huge budget for public music education, bringing kids from the inner city, from the suburbs, and other places to learn about music. Under the heading of Lincoln Center, there must be some creative work." They accepted his conditions, not just because they wanted him, but because his suggestions were good. The timing was fantastic, as contributors like the Rockefellers and others wanted to make a mark on the city.

I think his greatest musical influences are hard to assess, because it is difficult to see where music is going to go. For instance, Chopin had an incredibly wonderful, original style. But if you ask anyone if they were influenced by him, they would say no. The case with Schuman though—he really instituted what American music is, along with Copland, Roy Harris, and Samuel Barber. Copland went to Paris to study under Nadia Boulanger, but Roy Harris, William Schuman, Barber and Bernstein were all American-educated.

To those who wish to conduct his music, I would first say to study

5

several of his works. Get a feel for what he is all about—the character is quite direct, simple, and powerful.

For my fifth concert in New York, I received a mediocre review and brooded for a week. He came to me and said, "When they gave you amazing reviews—better than you even thought that you deserved, you didn't question it!" One of his comments to me was a masterpiece: "Don't believe the critics when they tell you that you are a genius. Because when they tell you that you are a dog, you can't ask, 'what do they know?'"

Two weeks after hearing this great quote from Schuman, his latest symphony was premiered with the New York Philharmonic. The reviews the next day were devastating. I've never seen them so vicious… but it was understandable. It came at a time when atonal and other disturbing music was in fashion, and Schuman's work was probably too musical to satisfy the trend. Anyhow, his piece received terrible reviews. I thought, after his wise comments to me that he wouldn't pay attention to them; however he did take it hard.

One has to develop a strong skin as a performing artist. The worst part about it is that more people read the reviews than actually hear the concert.

One thing that I can assure you of is that regardless of the criticism, it never occurred to William Schuman even for a split second to quit writing music. After a couple of weeks, he forgot about the whole damned thing.

– 2 –

VINCENT PERSICHETTI

When I conducted the world premiere of Vincent Persichetti's *Stabat Mater* at Carnegie Hall with the Collegiate Chorale, he attended all of the rehearsals with the chorus and orchestra. I kept asking him specific questions about certain spots - whether he had suggestions or wanted anything changed - but for the most part he was fine with everything as rehearsed. During the last on-stage rehearsal, when I turned to him and asked "Vincent, is that OK?" He yelled from the hall—"Abe, forget that I'm here now! The piece is yours!" He knew that in order to get a great performance out of a conductor, it was best if the performers weren't concerned about the composer's presence. Of course, Bernstein had the same kind of wisdom. It did not necessarily indicate whether or not he would enjoy the performance, but he knew that trying to control the process wouldn't yield better results.

I once had to prepare the Juilliard chorus and orchestra for a world premiere of Persichetti's *The Creation*. He came to one of my final rehearsals, and at some point I felt that I was finished, and had done everything in my power to prepare the piece. I turned to him and said, "Would you like to take over and conduct the rest of the rehearsal?" He very kindly refused and said, "No, no, you please finish the rehearsal," which I did. When I got off the podium and we went for coffee afterwards he admitted, "I was not ready to conduct the piece. I wrote the piece, I know the music, but as you know, you have to prepare to conduct it, to study it from the conductor's point of view and from the player's point of view in order to conduct it well. That's why I refused to take over the rehearsal." That gave me a very interesting insight into this man, who was highly trained as a pianist, a conductor, an organist, and a composer - a person who knew the conducting profession from the inside out. One of his greatest strengths was his understanding of his own capabilities. He was a versatile musician, and his attitude could have gone one of two ways: he could have had a vague idea about some of his talents, or the clear perspective that he had about his abilities in each of the separate disciplines. For all of his gifts as a composer, teacher, conductor and keyboard player, he had a correct and wonderful sense of humility about each. His legacy will of course be his composition. In an age where so many composers were confused as to whether they should write in the dodecaphonic (twelve tone) style or another that was fashionable at the time, my own observation is that Persichetti wrote what I call "real" music, not bending to the fashion of the day. Of course, only future generations will be able to judge the staying power of his music, but to me, of all his compositions that I am familiar with, the *Stabat Mater* was probably the most beautiful and profound. Like other meaningful choral works, the inspiration of the music parallels the depth of the text in that mysterious and powerful way. There are pieces of music that are beautiful, independent of their texts, and there are texts that are beautiful, independent of the music to which they are set; but when the inspiration of the musical invention dovetails the inspiration of the text, and the most profound words are set to the most beautifully moving music—that is where choral music becomes deep, moving and profound.

While Persichetti achieved this duality spectacularly, he was a man of great humility. Once we were sitting for coffee, and he had a score of Mozart in front of him. He showed me a passage of the music he was looking at and said, "If through all of my life I have written twelve measures that are as good as this, I will feel that my life was worthwhile."

LEONARD BERNSTEIN

Leonard Bernstein and Abraham Kaplan

"Musical down to his bone marrow." Both my father and grandfather used that expression when they encountered someone extremely musical. From the first moment I met Leonard Bernstein, the phrase immediately entered my mind. The man was music incarnate.

First Collaboration

During the summer of 1961, I was appointed Director of Choral Music at the Juilliard School. Prior to the beginning of the school year, I received a call from Mr. Bernstein's secretary, Helen Coats. Hearing of my appointment, Bernstein wanted to know if the Julliard chorus would be interested in collaborating with him and the New York Philharmonic in a performance of Bach's *St. Matthew Passion* at Carnegie Hall. I must tell you that the rest of my colleagues didn't look at Bernstein as the legend that he turned out to be—but I was already in awe of his genius, and was exhilarated at the thought of working with the Maestro. I responded that I would be honored to work with Maestro Bernstein, but that I would need to first check with my new bosses at Juilliard. To my great surprise and amazement, the dean actually rejected the request! To this day I do not understand his rationale—but since I had not even started my job there yet, I did not ask for an explanation. Nevertheless, I found a way to work on the project.

During that same summer I had also been selected as Director of the Collegiate Chorale,* a group that was started fifteen years earlier by Robert Shaw. The community chorus took its name from the venue in which it had originally rehearsed, the basement of the Marble Collegiate Church of New York. I decided to use the Collegiate Chorale in order to fulfill Mr. Bernstein's request, despite one significant challenge: this group, prior to my appointment, had dwindled from one hundred and fifty singers down to only fifty-seven—which would not be enough to perform the St. Matthew's Passion. To be honest, fifty-seven is an

---

* While the world is now familiar with many choruses that use "Chorale" in their group names, the Collegiate Chorale of New York was actually the first, named by Robert Shaw. William Schuman joked with me that when Robert Shaw established the group, he performed "one of the greatest crimes against the English language." He meant, of course, that Shaw reinterpreted "chorale" to mean something different than just a choral melody—as in "Bach Chorale"—and the music world has never been the same since.

overstatement, if it means that all of the members actually showed up at every rehearsal.

Never to be dissuaded in those years, I had enough Israeli chutzpah and youthful naiveté to think, "Bernstein's invitation is for the second part of the season—by that time, I can restore the Chorale to its original strength." I called back Helen Coats and told her about the Juilliard situation, and then about my other chorus, with which I would be happy to meet the Maestro's request. Perhaps it was fate - *Mrs.* Bernstein had been a member of the Chorale years earlier, and so Ms. Coats was aware of the group. Word had gotten out about the group's shrinkage though, so with a bit of surprise, she asked, "Is the Chorale still in existence? How many singers are there?" I boldly stated that the group was a hundred and fifty members strong (I had an instinct that whenever I was asked such a question, I *always* said "yes," and scrambled to find a way to make it so.).

Luckily, many of the people who sang with Robert Shaw came back when they heard that I was appointed as a permanent director, and we happily started the season with a hundred and twenty-five to a hundred and fifty singers. We were well prepared by the concert date, and that was the beginning of a delicious, sixteen-year musical partnership with Bernstein.

During our first piano rehearsal with Maestro Bernstein, I enjoyed one of my most rewarding experiences as a young conductor. Bernstein decided to "test" the Chorale on that particular day, and did something that showed me immediately that he had an understanding for conducting choruses. Bernstein told the Chorale when he stood in front of them, "I'm going to do an experiment. We will sing the chorale on page 191, but I will conduct it capriciously, arbitrarily changing the tempo." I knew right away that he wanted to see if the group could follow him. Even in those days, I used to rehearse choruses at varying tempi, so that they would be attentive to the conducting rather than drifting into autopilot…but I had never tested them at this level! When the Maestro got on the podium, he conducted the music with the most dramatic and erratic tempo changes, trying to throw the singers off track. Much to my delight they were absolutely perfect, and stayed with his every move. When it was over, the Maestro rewarded the group with an exaggerated hand gesture, as if he was trying to wipe glue off of his hand…as if to say, "all right already, you win!" Needless to say, I was beaming with happiness, and could not wipe the silly grin from my face. Years later, after preparing choruses for so many other conductors, it became a significant part of my mindset and routine to prepare the singers at the broadest range of tempi possible for a piece.

The final rehearsals for *The Passion* were in Carnegie Hall, and as the day grew nearer, Maestro Bernstein became more and more excited about the concert. When the performance was only a few days away, he suddenly asked me if I would do for him what he called a "big favor," which for me was a privilege. "You know," he said, "my father is an orthodox Jew. I have tried for years to get him to come and listen to the *St. Matthew Passion*, but he would never come. In years past, in Lawrence, Massachusetts, where he lived, he remembered the Irish Catholics in his neighborhood getting out of church at Easter time after hearing the Passion story, and stoning some of the Jewish-owned businesses." His father didn't want to hear the story that he thought was responsible for provoking such anti-Semitic behavior. "This time," continued Bernstein, "I told him that I had an Israeli preparing the choruses who shared my passion for the music…I told him that you would sit with him if he would just come and listen." To make a long story short, I met Bernstein Senior in the conductor's box, and there he confirmed for me his son's explanation. He was an absolutely delightful man with a wonderful sense of humor. He was moved not only by the music, but also by the story, which he had never heard before. At intermission, he leaned toward me and in Yiddish said, "even though it's a lie…it's a *beautiful* story." A recording was made of that performance by Columbia Records, and is now available on compact disc through Sony.

One evening, soon after I had met my future wife, I brought her to a rehearsal with Bernstein for a performance of Haydn's *The Creation*. She had heard only one classical concert in her lifetime before that, conducted by Herbert von Karjan in Carnegie Hall, and that was the extent of her knowledge about classical music. When Bernstein was rehearsing *The Creation*, after running through the first passage with the chorus, he asked them to sit at the beginning while they were singing text that says "and the spirit of God was hovering on the waters, and God said 'let there be light'" - and the chorus answers, "and there was light!" On the word, "light," Bernstein wanted the chorus to rise suddenly to their feet. *The Creation* was sung in German, and Bernstein knew that a lot of the singers who were so-called "purists" would be critical of him and call him "theatrical" for such staging. This was at the beginning of his career, when he was criticized for everything. Although I thought his choreography was a beautiful effect that needed no explanation, he justified it to the chorus, explaining, "When Haydn first wrote *The Creation*, the audience knew every word, and when the audience first heard this section of the music, they rose to their feet." What Haydn *did* do was create an extreme surprise within the music, at the point where God apparently switched the light on. For Bernstein, standing at this section was just punctuation to the already dramatic score. Haydn has the chorus sing in unison, on a single note for the words, "And there was…" unfolding the music into a loud and glorious C major chord on the word "LIGHT." Bernstein later tried to explain the entire series of events to my date, who hadn't the faintest idea what he was talking about—and I've never seen Bernstein so frustrated, either before or since that time—he so craved understanding and adoration. With respect to my future wife—I should have taken this as a bad sign, but that's another story!

Anyhow, when the rehearsal ended, he offered to drive us home. We walked out of the rehearsal hall, which was on one of the side streets of Times Square, and met his Lincoln limousine and driver. Much to our surprise, he said to us, "Let's take a walk—I'll buy you an Orange Julius," and told his driver, "Follow us." It was quite a comical event, being followed by a black Lincoln on our late night walking excursion across Times Square.

Bernstein & Mahler

Bernstein was known as an incredible interpreter of *all* Mahler symphonies, so when I was asked to prepare for him *Symphony No. 2* ("The Resurrection") by Mahler with the Collegiate Chorale, I was in for a treat. As usual, I said "Yes," and when he routinely asked how many people I would have in the Chorale, I told him that I thought we would have around a hundred and fifty.

While rehearsing for this performance, I encountered what some have called "the dark side" of Bernstein's personality. This wasn't my usual experience with him, although the media liked to talk about such things. In the middle of one joint rehearsal with the chorus and symphony, the Maestro suddenly stopped, and I noticed that he was upset. He said, "No, no good," but didn't specify what was wrong with what he had heard. Usually he was very specific and constructive when something displeased him, but this time he was pouting like a child, repeating "No, no good" over and over. I slowly approached the podium in order to see if I could figure out what the problem was. He again repeated "It's no good!" Finally, in an outburst, he revealed the cause of his apparent displeasure. "How many people do you have here?" he asked. When told that there were around a hundred and twenty-five singers on the stage, he retorted, "I knew it, it isn't the hundred and fifty that you promised me!" I was surprised at the outburst, because I hadn't seen that element of his personality before.

Although I was young and temperamental at the time, I responded very calmly and pragmatically to him. I was mainly worried about wasting rehearsal time, which would have an effect on the performance. In the beginning of the rehearsal, I was just waiting for his mood to "go away." Since it was the first time I had seen him act this way, I was patient—but I later heard of similar outbursts where he kept entire orchestras waiting for almost an hour. In this case everyone was waiting for him to explain specifically what he wanted, or to do something to change the performance. Putting my hand over my mouth to shield the chorus and orchestra from my words, I said, "Maestro, if you are unhappy with me, or don't like what I've prepared for you, just don't invite me to perform with you any more—but please, don't keep demoralizing the chorus like this, and taking up the rehearsal time…because it will hurt your performance." I assumed the Maestro could be persuaded on the basis of making the music better, and fortunately the tactic worked.

From my observation during that time together, I believe *The Resurrection* was his favorite symphony by Mahler. He not only performed this piece from memory, he even rehearsed it from memory. During one of the rehearsals in the previous weeks, he described to the cellos how to play a particularly luscious, wonderful phrase, and sang it. When the musical line dropped below the human vocal range, his voice cracked, and he cried out, "if only I could sing!" The entire chorus and orchestra burst into laughter…*as if he didn't have enough talents already!* The final performance was out of this world.

In one of Bernstein's Sunday afternoon subscription concerts he also chose to perform *The Resurrection*. After that performance I came backstage for the final bow as was customary. Besides being a great musician Bernstein was a showman and was always interested in knowing how everyone enjoyed the show. I've seen him come off stage many times, looking around to see who was there on that particular day or night, trying to discern what they thought of the concert. I thought that this particular performance was amazing—in fact it was the best performance I'd ever heard of *The Resurrection*. As I stood backstage waiting for him, I heard him mumbling to himself, "Today—it felt like I wrote the piece myself!" Believe me, the audience felt it too! By this time in our collaborations, I'd heard him conduct eight stunning performances of this symphony, and that afternoon concert was by far the most inspired. Hearing his words that day, I realized that the epitome of a good performance is not only for the conductor to *feel* as if he or she wrote the piece—it is as if he or she is actually writing it at that very moment, *while* conducting.

The 3rd ('Kaddish') Symphony

Jenny Tourel, Leonard Bernstein and Abraham Kaplan

17

In 1963, I received another call from Helen Coats, telling me, "Maestro Bernstein needs some advice." Several years before that, the Boston Symphony had commissioned him to write a symphony to celebrate its 75th anniversary. He was about eight years late in completing the commission, but was now finished and ready for the premiere performance.

The premise of the work took the Kaddish prayer, an orthodox Jewish prayer of mourning, and interjected narration into the music written by Bernstein himself. The piece is not what first comes to mind when thinking of a symphony, but neither were his first two symphonies. The first, subtitled *Lamentations of Jeremiah*, incorporated traditional synagogue cantilations, and was sung by an alto soloist. The second symphony, entitled *The Age of Anxiety*, was actually a piano concerto for all intents and purposes.

The *Kaddish Symphony* has purpose and cause, very much like *Mass* by Bernstein, written eight years later. *Mass* became very much what the *War Requiem* was for Benjamin Britten, who used the Catholic prayer for the dead overlaid with modern anti-war poetry. In the *Kaddish Symphony*, Bernstein used the traditional prayer for the dead, recited in Aramaic, as a backdrop for his own personal arguments with God. In one part of the symphony, the narrator cries out, *"Tin God! You who created the heaven and the earth and all of these galaxies—can't you put some order on this little speck, called earth?"* Despite the critics who thought the text was irreverent or even blasphemous, the principal of arguing with God was not only acceptable, but also welcomed in the orthodox Jewish tradition. For this and other personal reasons, Maestro Bernstein felt strongly that he wanted to do his world premiere of the *Kaddish Symphony* in Israel. Although the Boston Symphony had originally commissioned the piece, they graciously obliged and gave the Maestro their blessing.

Bernstein already had plans to visit Israel, as he had been invited to conduct a Tchaikovsky program with the Israeli Philharmonic. Since he had now finished his own symphony, he felt that this was the perfect opportunity to change the original program and instead conduct the *Kaddish* world premiere.

The Israeli Philharmonic quickly responded to Bernstein's request, saying that they did not have a chorus in Israel capable of singing his difficult music. Knowing that I had recently come from Israel, Bernstein had Ms. Coats contact me to ask if I had any suggestions. I suggested that the Professional Radio Chorus in Jerusalem and the Conservatory Chorus in Tel Aviv collaborate, and that together the choruses should be able to perform the piece.

After several weeks I received another call from Ms. Coats, this time explaining, "Lenny has just heard back from the Israeli Philharmonic. While they understand your suggestion, they say that they don't have anybody who can prepare this kind of difficult music. So Lenny is asking if you would be willing to go and prepare it." I was thrilled and agreed on the spot, offering to stay with my family and to do the work for free if the Philharmonic was willing to take care of my travel expense to Israel. The project would take a long time, but Juilliard encouraged teachers to do such international tours, because the exposure and "professional" status of their faculty was such a large part of the school's stature.

Several more weeks passed and I didn't hear anything, nor did I receive my tickets in the mail. The performance date was drawing nearer and nearer. Suddenly, I received a call from Helen Coats, reporting that the Israeli Philharmonic was asking for my whereabouts! I was shocked, because I had heard nothing, and assumed that the performance had been cancelled. The scenario that was emerging confounded Bernstein. He asked me, "What the hell is happening there? I don't understand their problem…I am offering them a world premiere—one that *should* belong to the Boston Symphony - and they don't seem to want it. Do you really think they don't want to perform my music?"

It became clear to me that the Israeli Philharmonic had been trying to dissuade Maestro Bernstein for several reasons. I explained to him that as unbelievable as it sounded, the group was a co-operative, probably focusing on how much more money they would make if they could convince him to conduct an all Tchaikovsky program. The classics always made money in Israel, and the Philharmonic usually repeated these same programs nine or ten times. I explained, "Maestro Bernstein, if they do your symphony, they will have to hire more musicians, have more rehearsals—they just don't have the imagination…what can I tell you?" I speculated too that the subject matter of Bernstein's symphony, and perhaps the fact that it was written in Aramaic concerned the Israeli Philharmonic with respect to attracting its largely secular audience. Bernstein, hearing this, decided aloud that he would *not* go to Israel, and would definitely not conduct Tchaikovsky for the Israeli Philharmonic.

A week after that conversation—as if by a miracle—I received my airline tickets in the mail. I gave Bernstein a call to tell him, but cautioned, "These choruses are not going to be able to prepare in such a short time frame." They had waited until almost no time remained to rehearse for the concert. The Maestro said to me, "I understand what you are saying…but are you still willing to go and try?" I was willing to do whatever it took in order to make this dream come true and gladly obliged the Maestro's wish. I would try my best with the short time available, and we decided that I would call him to discuss the group's progress throughout the weeks ahead. "If you think they will not be ready, then I will cancel my trip," he told me.

Before I left the United States, Bernstein was still putting the finishing touches on the symphony, and I received each section of the score as it was completed. When he got to the end of the piece, however, I noticed that every few days I would receive a changed version of the ending—and none was very different from the one before it. The changes were so small, and copying was so expensive at the time that I couldn't understand what he was doing. I still didn't know him particularly well, having only collaborated with him on two prior projects, and this was the first collaboration that involved his own music. Finally I decided to call, and asked respectfully, "I have received several versions of the end for your *Kaddish Symphony*...may I ask why you are continuing to make revisions?" I explained to him that all of the versions thus far were beautiful, and could work nicely with the previous music. He was apparently frustrated that such a major symphonic piece was ending quietly. "I am very unhappy with the ending," he exclaimed.

After considering his words, I felt moved to encourage him. I thought that his instinct to end softly was right for the piece, and communicated as much, saying that I believed his integrity as a composer would not allow him to patch on an ending that didn't belong in the music. I urged him to consider other profound pieces of music in the choral repertoire—Beethoven's *Missa Solemnis*, the *Requiem* by Giuseppe Verdi—profound works that end quietly. The *Missa Solemnis* has a rather perfunctory ending. One can almost hear Beethoven say to his audience, "Go home, I have said what I had to say." In the Verdi *Requiem*, after one of the most amazing buildups (dynamically) in all of symphonic literature, Verdi concludes the piece with a whisper on the words, *"Libera me."* Bernstein's *Kaddish Symphony*, a virtual argument with the Almighty, was similarly profound, and deserved a similarly sobering end. In the *Kaddish*, he was writing about the state of the world. Whether because of that conversation or some other turn of events, Bernstein was apparently satisfied, and I did not receive any further revisions.

When I arrived in Israel, no one waited to welcome me at the airport, as the Philharmonic usually did for visiting conductors. "A prophet is never welcome in his hometown," I told myself, smiling. The next morning when I went to the Philharmonic offices, they were actually surprised to see me. It became clear that they had intentionally waited for what they thought was too long, expecting me not to come. I began right away, taking the initiative to organize the two necessary choruses, both of whom were thrilled at the opportunity to work on the piece. We found a venue and a wonderful accompanist, and we proceeded to work our tails off, with me traveling from Tel Aviv to Jerusalem several times a week. On Saturdays, we brought the entire Jerusalem chorus to Tel Aviv for a joint rehearsal, and worked six to eight hours together. When it came closer to the actual performance date, Bernstein called to ask if I thought the chorus was ready, but I sadly had to tell him "no." He decided to come anyhow as planned, hoping for whatever improvement possible, and to make his own judgment about the group's preparedness. If they were truly unable to perform, he would return to the United States and give up on the whole idea.

Bernstein quickly arrived in Israel and attended our joint chorus rehearsal. By then I knew his routine—he asked me to conduct the entire piece for him, so that he could listen. Never before and never since then have I seen him look the way he looked after hearing that group sing. Usually, no matter how much he liked or didn't like a run-through, he always told the chorus, "It was wonderful," or something to that effect, and started working on the specific things that he wanted to change or incorporate into the music. He simply couldn't fake delight this time—in some parts of the music, the chorus really sounded quite horrible. When I finished conducting, I gestured toward the podium, and said, "Maestro, it's your turn."

Bernstein took the podium slowly and with his face down, started working very, very hard with the chorus. As I mentioned earlier, he knew very well how to work with singers. He went through many of the same things that the accompanist and I had gone through over the previous weeks, rolling up his sleeves and getting to work.

Nine performances were scheduled, and in spite of the trials and tribulations of preparing for the events, the Israeli Philharmonic and the chorus gave nine world-class performances to sold-out crowds. Bernstein was so absolutely commanding in his presence and passion for the music that every concert was magical, and the delighted crowds offered long, standing ovations.

In some ways, the experience confirmed for me what I have long believed about choruses—that the voices together make up a single, unique instrument, only as expressive as the conductor that is "playing" them. Regardless of their own lack of ability in this particular instance, in Bernstein's masterful hands the result was extremely moving. In the same way, I would rather hear Itzhak Perlman play a twenty dollar violin than hear a poor musician play a Stradivarius. Although this chorus was not of the quality that either Bernstein or I would have liked, in the end, the audience heard nothing but Maestro Bernstein— and in that, overlooked the flaws in the instrument that he played. Back in the United States, after subsequently recording the *Kaddish* with my Camerata Singers and the New York Philharmonic, Bernstein mentioned that he had received a tape of the Israeli performance. He said to me, "Was it really that bad?" I said, "Yes!" "Then why was it so exciting?" he asked. My response, "You got used to the sound of this crummy instrument!"

The *Chichester Psalms*

Leonard Bernstein and Abraham Kaplan

Two years after the world premiere of the *Kaddish* Symphony, I had the great privilege and pleasure of collaborating again with Maestro Bernstein on the world premiere of his *Chichester Psalms*. Every summer the Cathedral of Chichester, in Sussex, England, collaborated with its neighbors to produce a music festival, for which Leonard Bernstein was commissioned to write these Psalms in 1965.

As Bernstein was finishing the score, he invited me to his apartment to listen to the music. He sat at the piano and played portions of the score for me, and I was absolutely thrilled with what I heard. He also told me an interesting anecdote about how he developed the music on a few of the sections. One of the most fascinating explanations pertained to the middle section of the second movement, which is based on Psalm 23 (*The Lord is My Shepherd*) and interjects portions of Psalm 2 (*Why Do the Nations Rage?*). In the music, Psalm 2 interrupts the tranquility of the Twenty-third Psalm. Literally translated, "why do nations rage," the "Lamah Rag'shu Goyim" text is sung to very agitated and explosive music, employing shouts and unusual percussion instruments, like the frusta (whip). Bernstein explained that although one might expect him to compose violent music to accompany the nations raging against God, he actually pulled the texture of this music from something completely different. He said, "You know, I took an entire year on sabbatical from the New York Philharmonic to write a musical, but the musical never came to fruition. Some of the music that made its way into the *Chichester Psalms* was salvaged from a section in that work that was very similar to the gang fight scene in *West Side Story*."

To my great delight Bernstein salvaged another piece of music from the same abandoned musical, and dedicated it to the Camerata Singers and myself. The piece was entitled, *Warmup*, and became the opening number for a series of Symphonic Choral Society concerts that I performed with the Camerata Singers and Camerata Symphony Orchestra over several years at Avery Fischer Hall. Eventually, the same piece also made its way into the *Mass* that Bernstein wrote years later.

Once I received a copy of the full *Chichester Psalms* score, I became more and more excited about the prospect of its publication. I came to the conclusion that this was a definitive Bernstein masterpiece, and the next time that I was with him, I told him as much. "I think this piece will live forever, and will be played after both of us are gone…probably the most of any of your other compositions," I boldly proclaimed. Bernstein argued vigorously that I was exaggerating, and that this was just a small, eighteen and a half minute piece that was good, but nothing special. While he may have hoped that I was right in my assessment, it is possible that he didn't appreciate the greatness of the piece. As one can see many times throughout history, composers often least appreciate their most popular and accessible compositions, and often dote on the ones that audiences appreciate the least. George Frideric Handel, for example, complained bitterly about receiving so many compliments (and ticket requests) for *Messiah*, claiming that his opera, *Martha*, was really a much better composition. Composer, Darius Milhaud once said to me, "You know, composers are like mothers—they protect their weakest children." In the case of the *Chichester Psalms*, Bernstein was *under*estimating his strongest child.

Those friendly "arguments" between us continued up until the day of the performance. On the Sunday prior to the performance, I read an article in the New York Times, in which Bernstein summarized a whole series of concerts of contemporary music that he had finished performing with the New York Philharmonic. It included practically every style of contemporary music at the time, and his comments can today be found in a book called *Findings*. After he wrote about the many contemporary pieces of music in the series, he jotted down a few words about his newly-completed *Chichester Psalms*, introducing them for his upcoming performance later that week. He concluded his article with a short poem, in which he referred to the *Chichester Psalms* as his "youngest child."

When Bernstein came to conduct his first piano rehearsal, he came in during the second movement which includes the Twenty-third Psalm, in the section where the sopranos are divided in two, singing a canon. Upon hearing it for the first time, he exclaimed, "I want you to sing that section so that you sound like the Supremes." The group was so popular at the time that the choir knew instinctively what Bernstein wanted. Through this little bit of coaching, Bernstein revealed not only his versatility as a musician, but also the extent of his involvement and interest in the popular music of the day.

Three months after that world premiere performance with the New York Philharmonic, the America Israel Foundation asked me to conduct the *Chichester Psalms* with my Camerata Singers for their annual fundraising event. The America Israel Foundation was an organization that raised scholarship money for Israeli students coming to the United States, of which I had been a beneficiary when I first attended Juilliard. They asked me how much it would cost for the Camerata Singers to do this performance, and while I offered my own services for free, there was a union minimum that was required for them to pay each singer. Therefore, I needed to figure out the smallest number of singers necessary to have a successful performance. With the New York Philharmonic performance, I had used one hundred singers, which I knew wouldn't be necessary, but I wanted to ask Maestro Bernstein for his opinion on the subject. I vaguely remember that they asked if I could do it with thirty. So I called Bernstein and explained the situation. He was a shrewd negotiator, and knew the realities of dealing with the business side of the music world. He knew better than to designate a required number of singers, and instead said, "Ask for sixty, and settle for forty."

The Maestro brought his wife and two children to that performance, as he loved to hear others perform his music. When the entire family came backstage after the concert, he said something to me like, "Wonderful!" Pretending to be jealous, he continued, "...and from memory too!" He was absolutely graceful and full of humility when it came to encouraging other musicians in those ways. And while he was welcome at my rehearsals, he never attended them or tried to control the outcome of a performance in any way. He had great instincts, and knew that in order to get the best performance out of an ensemble, it would be best if the performers didn't worry about the composer's presence or thoughts about their performance.

Over time, I persisted in my enthusiasm about the *Chichester Psalms*, and at one point said to Bernstein, "The language barrier might be the only hindrance to seeing this composition become your most popular concert piece in our lifetime." The entire piece was written in Hebrew, because that was how Bernstein remembered reading the psalms as a child. Although he didn't speak the modern language, it was most meaningful to him when he thought about the text in Hebrew. "Therefore," I continued, "if I may suggest, when you publish the music, why don't you also include a singable English translation, and state your preference that it be performed in Hebrew?" He agreed to try it as an experiment, and asked me as a speaker of both languages to work on the suggested English translation.

I enthusiastically took to the task of preparing an English version, but found it quite difficult. The structure of the two languages is quite different, most notably in the number of syllables and the placement of the accents within each phrase. For example, the Twenty-third Psalm begins with,

"The Lord is my shep-herd, I shall not want."

1   **2**   3   4   **5**   6   7   **8**   9   **10**

(10 syllables, numbers in bold are emphasized)

In Hebrew, the same sentence is as follows:

"A-do-nai ro-i, lo eh sar."

1   **2**   **3**   4   **5**   **6**   7   **8**

(8 syllables, numbers in bold are emphasized)

I tried my best, working from the poetic King James translation of the Bible, but found it immensely difficult. After I prepared the best version that I could, Bernstein invited me to his house in the country so we could review and work on the English together. While he complemented me that I spoke both languages, his English was definitely better than mine, and more literary. We worked, I believe, something like six hours on the project with one lunch break, and at some point he was so exhausted that he said, "Forget it." I think he was also dissatisfied with the results. He said, "Forget it, if they don't want to perform it in Hebrew, let them not perform it." Again I was confronted by this wonderful quality that Bernstein had when it came to his compositions. As with the *Kaddish Symphony*, where his integrity as a musician wouldn't let him patch on an unnaturally big ending, Bernstein refused to compromise the music of the *Chichester Psalms* just for the sake of translation. Of course he would have liked to sell the work sooner rather than later—not only for the monetary reward, but to see the success of his "child," during his own lifetime. Still, he remained steadfast in his belief that singing the work in English would have diminished its quality.

It is possible that Bernstein did not appreciate the *Chichester Psalms* as much as he did the *Kaddish Symphony* because it was simply a much shorter work. He labored much more on the *Kaddish Symphony* and perhaps as a result was much more attached to the music. Even before his passing, however, the *Chichester Psalms* came to enjoy the greatest recognition of all Bernstein's choral compositions, and I've always cherished the fact that he was able to enjoy its great popularity with audiences around the world.

− 4 −

FRANK SINATRA

When the Histadrut—Israel's association of trade unions—decided to celebrate its fortieth anniversary in Madison Square Garden, it asked Frank Sinatra to emcee the event. He was to narrate the history of the organization, and at the beginning of each of its four decades, to sing a song that he had popularized during that era. I was invited to be the conductor of the symphony orchestra, accompanying Sinatra and other musical acts in the show.

I clearly remember one of Sinatra's songs, "A Foggy Day in London Town". I was quite nervous about it. While I had no problem conducting symphonic or other classical and popular sheet music, I had no idea how to conduct a "chart." Charts are written without exact musical notation, but with more flexibility. They are somewhat improvised, with a certain order. I knew the principles behind them, but had no idea how to conduct them.

The moment I was given my assignment, I ran to the music store and asked for several different versions of the sheet music. I purchased four records, because each of the four songs was on a different one. I put the records on, opened the sheet music…but lo and behold, I could barely see a connection between the two! Not only was there no connection between the performance and the printed notes, but there was no correlation to when and where the singer came in.

I panicked. To make things worse, I was told that I would not be able to see Mr. Sinatra until the afternoon of the concert, for the first and only rehearsal, and that his accompanist would bring the parts for the orchestra.

I told the contractor to make sure he hired musicians that could not only play symphonic music, but could play charts.

Finally the moment came, and when the star showed up, I said "Mr. Sinatra, I must tell you that I've conducted many things, but I've never conducted a chart, and I would really appreciate it if...."

He interrupted me with a tap on the shoulder, and said, "Don't worry kid—you'll be OK". Trusting in his genius, I decided I would just keep conducting, and hope for the best.

The rehearsal began, I conducted...and he came in. I conducted until the fermata, where I stopped and held the note. When it felt logical, I continued, and everything went fine.

When we came to certain points of the songs, Sinatra asked the orchestra for particular sounds, and the experience was wonderful.

The stage was huge—there was room for a symphonic orchestra and a forty-person troupe of dancers. He was on one side of the stage, and we were on the other. When the performance began, I would start the intro of the orchestra while he walked across the stage, and when the intro was finished, he would turn toward the audience and begin singing the song.

You know how casual he is, even in movies—so Frank Sinatra. The parts are made for him. This occasion was no exception—when he narrated, he had a wonderful casual way of speaking.

The most amazing thing about this man occurred to me during that performance. I think I finally understood why he was such a great artist. The split second before he began to sing, he appeared to go into self-hypnosis. Since he was just a few feet from me, I realized how blue his eyes were—and he sang each song as if it was the first time in his life. This was not just for show, either—the first row of the audience was a half mile away from us, so I was really the only one who could see how the music transformed him.

When I witnessed this man performing each song as if it was the first time, I knew then that he would be popular until the last day of his life and beyond. Many have also noted the mastery of Sinatra's phrasing and his ability to "tell a story" with his singing, but to me, it was his ability to make every performance seem like his first that gave his artistry its lasting quality.

IGOR STRAVINSKY

Igor Stravinsky and Abraham Kaplan

As a person and as a musician, Stravinsky was *delicious*—simply a wonderful, genuine personality without a false or pretentious bone in his body. This was the case when I met him, which was when he was older and more mature, but I have a suspicion that he had always been that way. Born in Russia, he spent a lot of time in Paris writing music for the Ballet Russe, a Russian ballet company. He wrote some of his favorite works there, many of which are pieces for dance. He was also tremendously influenced by his friendship with the Russian choreographer, Diaghilev. He asked to be buried in the same cemetery in Venice as his friend, who died fifty years earlier.

One of the most amazing stories about Stravinsky was about the time that his most famous composition, *The Rite of Spring*, was performed in Paris. When the performance was over, the entire audience rose to its feet—but half was cheering and half was booing! In retrospect, that particular piece of music has been declared by many as the most important piece of music written in the twentieth century.

I met and got to know Stravinsky when I was asked to prepare all of the choral pieces at the Stravinsky festival, organized one summer by the New York Philharmonic. The director of the festival was Lukas Foss, a wonderful musician whom Stravinsky adored. Bernstein was also friends with Lukas Foss, and because of the mutual admiration between Foss and Stravinsky, Foss was put in charge of the festival. I think that year's founding festival was entitled *"Stravinsky and his contemporaries— those who influenced him and those whom he influenced."*

He did not come to the entire festival, but came for the end, with the assignment of conducting the final work, his popular *Symphony of Psalms*. There were some rumors among musicians that he was not such a good conductor, and that he couldn't really hear what was happening in the orchestra—but there were two incidents that proved the critics wrong.

Stravinski and I were sitting and following the score of *Oedipus Rex* while Lukas Foss was conducting. We were listening to a section that ended with a double bass solo, holding softly the note, F. The Maestro suddenly shouted, "F sharp!" When I asked him where the F sharp was supposed to be, he said, "In the trill of the clarinet." I pointed out that it was not in the music, and he said, "Anyone who knows my music knows that I'm not going to trill E-F-E-F when there is already an F sustained—so it is obviously a mistake and should be an F Sharp." In other words, an F sharp was needed in the clarinet trill to make it heard against the F in the bass. It gave me a basis for understanding the logic of his writing. From that point forward, if I saw something like that again, and it sounded strange, I knew to say, "Maybe the sharp was left out of the manuscript."

As we became more and more friendly, I recall another enlightening experience. In a festival concert, to be conducted by Ernest Ansermet, I prepared a piece that Stravinsky wrote which only lasts about nine or ten minutes, but which also employs a tremendously large orchestra. The piece is titled *Le roi des étoiles* (in Russian *Zvedolikii*) and it describes Jesus as one whose face shines like the stars in heaven. The dedication reads "Hommage à Debussy." I don't remember if he wrote it in response to a composition contest held by the Debussy society, but he wrote it with a feel and sense of Debussy's music. The piece employs a male chorus, singing in Russian, and a huge orchestra of more than a hundred and twenty people—and you quickly realize that you have to hire extra people to do it for a performance. It is very, very difficult, because the language is difficult, and because the chorus usually sings in one meter while the orchestra is split into two different meters. Nevertheless, it is notated in such a way that it is possible, but difficult. I had read that Ansermet, who had recorded most of Stravinsky's work and written about it in his memoirs, had said that this was one piece that "could not be performed"—he believed it was physically impossible. In fact, when Ansermet came to perform the piece in New York City he was so nervous that he begged to attend my chorus rehearsals. He promised that he would just sit, listen and not say anything. The piece was very difficult for the chorus, but I had figured out how to prepare and rehearse it in a way that would help them learn and sing the complicated rhythms and the Russian text. I answered Ansermet, "Maestro, you can come to the second rehearsal." I knew that I would need the first rehearsal to myself, and I suspected he wouldn't be able to keep from interrupting. I assured him, "You will not have to give them any cues…all you will have to do is beat the time. They will come in correctly." When he eventually conducted, he couldn't help himself, and occasionally he tried to give some of the cues to the chorus—incorrectly. Fortunately, the chorus and orchestra ignored him at these junctures, and performed this amazing piece beautifully.

When Stravinsky came for the end of the festival, I asked him about the obscurities of the Russian poem. I told him I had two coaches for the Russian text. One of them was very good with the diction and the authenticity of the Russian sounds. The other was a very literary person from whom I wanted as literal a translation as possible, so that I would know the meaning of the words over the music. I told him that neither of these translators could explain one of the sentences…. and before I finished telling him about it, he said, "I didn't understand it either." He looked at my face and saw that as a young fan of his genius, I was wondering how someone could set text to music without understanding it. He said, "When I decide to set a poem to music, the words don't matter to me—it is the general atmosphere, it is the images." I suddenly realized, and this explained to me the text settings in many of his other works, that his attitude towards text was not much different from Bach's. Whatever the individual words in the poem, they were simply building blocks to Stravinsky in a larger construction.

My last episode with him was a concert that included three pieces. The first was the piece that was written by him for CBS television, called

The Flood. The second piece was his *Symphony in Three Movements*, and the last was *Symphony of Psalms.* The arrangement was that in this final concert, Robert Craft, his assistant, would conduct the first two compositions, and Stravinsky would conduct the *Symphony of Psalms* to close the festival. But at that time there was an airline strike and Robert Craft could not make it to New York from California. Hence, after Stravinsky attended my rehearsal for the two pieces that had chorus, he asked Lukas Foss who should conduct the symphony rehearsal in Craft's absence. Lukas Foss asked, "Did you see Abe Kaplan conduct? Did you like him?" When he answered, "Yes," Foss suggested that he ask me to conduct the rehearsal.

Stravinsky approached me and asked, "Do you know my *Symphony in Three Movements?*" to which I answered, "Yes." Actually, this was a slight exaggeration. The only exposure I had to the Symphony was when I had studied it many years prior at the conservatory in Israel. Obviously, that night I didn't sleep, and drank a lot of coffee. The next morning I conducted the rehearsal and had such fun! Stravinsky, however, was quite mischievous. When I was rehearsing the *Symphony of Psalms*, and felt that the orchestra and chorus were playing splendidly, I leaned over and said, "Maestro, is this ready?" He asked, "Is there anything else that you want to do?" A bit unsure of myself, I said, "Yes," just in case I missed something. He said, "Go ahead". This repeated itself twice, and I suddenly noticed that all of the orchestra members looked anxious, because we were running out of rehearsal time.

Finally, I just turned around and said "Maestro, they are ready." I walked down from the podium, through the hall, and in the semi-darkness we passed each other—he had eyes like burning coals. He leaned slightly toward me and with a big wink he said, "Now they'll watch me very carefully." He knew what he was doing. He mounted the podium and put his left hand on his hip. With his right hand he flicked his wrist, and it was the greatest performance of that piece that I have ever heard and will probably ever hear in my lifetime.

The reason that Stravinsky always conducted that way was that the angular part of his movement was so befitting his own music. Musicians don't just follow the beat—they actually move and breathe with him.

For others who conducted his music, there were two main things that Stravinsky wanted. First he would tell you to study the music to the point where you thought you wrote it yourself—so that it came out of you naturally, and with conviction…but in the process, he didn't want you to improve on it, nor to try to make changes. He wanted you to play *exactly* what you saw on the page. He was in complete reaction to the Romantic Period.

As a person, at least when I met him, he was known to be quite sarcastic—but I never experienced it with people that he appreciated musically, and who he didn't think were phony. When he dealt with me, it was all business, and also when he dealt with Foss, with whom he had a lifelong friendship, I found him to be one of the kindest men I had ever met. Kind, sweet, and warm—as I said in the beginning of the chapter, *delicious.*

I thought of Stravinski one night when I was standing in line at the Carnegie Deli after a performance, and I was wearing my coat and tails. Suddenly a man stormed out of the restaurant and screamed at me "I'm not taking this table if it is the last thing I do!" At that moment, I remembered a famous Stravinsky quote, that the only ones who still wear tails to work are the doormen and the maitre d'! He had said this as a witty admonition to musicians, reminding us that "we're in the service business."

– 6 –

AARON COPLAND

One of the choruses I prepared in New York was for a concert, conducted by Leonard Bernstein, which included a large choral piece on the same program as a Copland work for orchestra only. Aaron Copland came to some of the rehearsals, and as he sat in one of them, he suddenly heard the part of the rehearsal with the chorus. He turned to me with enormous surprise in his voice, and exclaimed, "Wow, choruses are terrific today!" I looked at him questioningly, wondering, "Why the surprise?" Copland explained that from early on in his childhood he had decided that he didn't like choral music. He said, "I used to escape from the auditoriums whenever there was a choral piece." His explanation was that when the orchestra played, everything sounded clean and clear, and when the chorus came in it always sounded to him like a "muddy blob" of sound.

So I asked him, "Is that the reason why you haven't written too much for chorus?" I pushed the issue… "And now you see that it can be as clear as instrumental music, right? Why don't you write something for us now?" Copland dodged the issue, saying that he had no text to compose to. I offered to send him some text, and asked if he would consider doing it. You see, at the time I was only a conductor. When you are only a conductor, you want to help the most important part of the music world, the composers, to flourish and create beautiful music.

I also learned later from introductions to some of his a cappella pieces that his teacher, Nadia Boulanger in Paris, was trying to encourage him to write choral music. And she had apparently come across the same resistance.

As for his personality, Copland was such a down-to-earth musician, a craftsman who just went about his business, which happened to be music. Much of his music feels like that—it is not romantic, expressive, or personal—although beautiful in many ways. His compositions were more like Stravinsky's music than those of Verdi, who wrote so much out of his own emotions.

– 7 –

PIERRE BOULEZ

Pierre Boulez is an honest man and one without a bone of guile in his body. As the music world knows, Boulez is not interested in any of the classical and romantic repertoire of the symphonic world. He tends to be interested in contemporary music, and the more experimental the better. During his youth, he even demonstrated against Stravinsky, who I guess he felt wasn't advanced or revolutionary enough. When Boulez became a conductor in London, however, and later the music director of the New York Philharmonic, he was required to do more traditional pieces - at least every so often. If Boulez refused, New York audiences knew how to rebel by not showing up. Even so, when he had to conduct something by a classical composer, Boulez would always try to perform an unknown piece by that person. In order to take classical music out of the "ivory tower," when he became director of the New York Philharmonic, he quickly changed the dress code, getting rid of the tails and making it a bit less formal.

So there he was, conducting a rehearsal of a Brahms symphony, and conducting it at a tempo that was absolutely wrong, not to mention impossible to play. The first cellist came to the podium and whispered, "Maestro, we usually play this in a much slower tempo." Here, Boulez demonstrated his characteristic humility—he replied to the cellist, "OK, thank you," and appropriately adjusted his speed.

When I worked with him, he chose to perform a well-known Stravinsky piece, and he also selected a very obscure Haydn mass. I finished preparing the chorus, knowing that he was arriving on a plane from Europe and would then come directly to the piano rehearsal. When he arrived, I saw him open a big volume, in which there were several scores of Haydn masses. I just assumed that he bought a volume of the masses so that he would not have to buy every mass separately. I didn't pay much attention to it at first. He conducted the Stravinsky piece and was very happy with it. Then he announced, "Let's do the Haydn." He opened the volume of Haydn masses, and we started reading through it together. One of Haydn's musical characteristics is sudden *fortes* and *pianos* in unexpected places. For example, in some masses, he will have a sudden *forte* (loud) and *fermata* (hold) on a word like, "*et*" (and). I noticed that while Boulez was going through the rehearsal he kept missing these dynamics. Then at some point, as he was turning pages and obviously reading them closely, two of the pages stuck together. It turned out that this volume had never been opened. He took something like a letter opener, separated the pages, opened it, turned the page, and said "continue."

Boulez' honesty came through that day, not in his choice of repertoire, but in how he responded when it became obvious that he had never studied the piece. Most famous conductors with huge egos would not only cover up their mistake, but would keep rehearsing the piece until they learned it themselves. Boulez, on the other hand, when he finished going through it said, "Thank you," and dismissed the chorus early.

He has a superb ear, and was able to use his mind to rehearse the difficult parts of music very, very well. His main interest was in composing, and eventually he pursued that part of his career more fully.

He now heads a very prestigious institute of composition, sponsored by the French government in Paris.

A true gentleman, he is very businesslike and austere—a very different personality than most artists.

THE COLLEGIATE CHORALE, ABRAHAM KAPLAN, CONDUCTOR, **BLOCH:SACRED SERVICE & MENNIN: THE CYCLE** (4THSYMPHONY) CARNEGIE HALL,SAT. DEC.19,1964,8:30 P.M. EPHRAIM BIRAN,SOLOIST

FOR MAIL ORDERS SEE REVERSE

– 8 –

ERNEST & SUZANNE BLOCH

When I came to Juilliard to study, I also applied for an assistantship in the ear-training department in solfege. Suzanne Bloch was the head of that department, and also the head of the Renaissance music department. I was granted the assistantship, and we consequently developed a wonderful friendship. I met her husband and her two sons. One of my first questions was whether she was related to the famous Ernest Bloch, and she explained that he indeed was her father. Over time, she began to tell me that she thought we would hit it off in an amazing way.

She called him one day and put us on the phone together, and we started talking. We spoke again several times after that. After my studies at Juilliard (I studied there for 4 years) I decided to return to Israel and renew my career there. One of the first concerts that I gave in Israel with the Radio chorus, the Conservatory Chorus and the Radio Orchestra was Bloch's Sacred Service.

Two weeks before the performance, I looked at the daily newspaper and saw a picture of Bloch, with the headline saying "Prominent Swiss Jewish Composer, Ernest Bloch is dead." It was as if something hit me over the head, telling me how stupid a person I was for not having gone to meet him while he was alive. That was when I thought, since music is so important to me—and since the great composers are the ones that supply me with the music that I am going to spend my LIFE with—I will never let that happen again. I missed that opportunity, but one of the things that I realize when I look back on my life is that although I made many mistakes, I rarely repeated them twice.

Ernest Bloch was the Director of the Conservatory of Music in Cleveland, and a wonderful teacher. While he was teaching the concerto grosso form, instead of just teaching the subject and telling stories about the form, he actually wrote one as an example, and it is a wonderful twentieth century masterpiece. It was very much like Prokofiev, who wrote the *Classical Symphony* to depict what Mozart or Haydn would have written if they had lived in the twentieth century.

His daughter, Suzanne, was a delightful musician in her own right—a professor at Juilliard, she played the recorder, the lute, and a variety of other old instruments very well. One of my most endearing memories of Suzanne is the way that she used to post a quotation on her office door at Juilliard every day, or at least once a week. I'm quite sure that she collected them herself, rather than taking them from a book of quotations, and I believe she sourced them from a wide variety of people. I found myself passing by her door often, just to read the recent post.

Suzanne was the first one who shocked me into realizing that all of those names that are on musical scores, like Bach, Beethoven, Mozart—were real people. Yes, it would seem obvious, but she is the one that brought the reality home to me. We were sitting one day having coffee, and she said to me, "You know, when I was sitting with Ravel in a coffee house in Paris…" I don't even remember the rest of the sentence, because I was so stunned by the first part. I had thought of Ravel as a name on a score, not as someone that sat with you and had coffee! I believe that was my first awakening to the fact that musicians are real people. It occurred to me then that if I ever had a chance to work with the century's greatest musicians, I should take it.

– 9 –

SEIJI OZAWA

Seiji Ozawa with Abraham Kaplan

I first met Ozawa when he was an assistant to Bernstein. He was one of the winners of a conducting competition, and as part of the prize he was given the opportunity to serve as an assistant to the New York Philharmonic. I met him when I prepared *The Passion According to St. Matthew*, my first Collegiate Chorale performance with the New York Philharmonic.

Later, Ozawa came to the New York Philharmonic as a guest conductor and chose *Jeanne d'Arc au Bûcher* (Joan of Arc at the Stake) by Honegger. This work used the chorus a lot as well, so I had the pleasure of working with him agan.

There weren't many Japanese conductors at that time who were raised in the Western tradition. His job as director of the Boston Symphony is probably one of the top five jobs in the United States. He is extremely talented and has a wonderful memory—he has conducted many, many scores from memory, and he has conducted them very *well* from memory.

His concert as guest conductor of the New York Philharmonic was a tour de force. As far as I'm concerned, that piece is *impossible* to memorize. He conducted it from memory, and it was just stunning. He was very pleasant to work with, and was fortunately delighted with my chorus at the time, the Camerata Singers. He is a rare conductor whose conducting is superbly clear, with or without a baton.

The main thing that I believe students should learn from Seiji Ozawa is how hard one should study a score, regardless of one's natural talent. I have a feeling that Ozawa keeps learning and learning. He is most in his element when conducting the big orchestral repertoire of the romantic period, because he brings them to full fruition. You can feel through his work that his soul is in Western music.

– 10 –

LEOPOLD STOKOWSKI

Working with Stokowski was really a marvelous experience. Years after he retired from Philadelphia, he started an orchestra in New York made up of freelance musicians, Julliard graduates, and a collection of other musicians. People who attended the first rehearsal marveled at something which proved to be very interesting: They recognized "the Stokowski sound" in the very first notes that came out of this orchestra and marveled how a new orchestra could produce such a unique sound. When he was music director in Philly, people thought it had more to do with the players and the quality of players. When he started a new orchestra, they couldn't believe that this sound was immediately transferred to eighty new people.

This is a great illustration—the conductor, wittingly or unwittingly, affects the quality of sound. Not so much by what he or she says, but by how he or she moves. When an orchestra is not just following a conductor from beat to beat—they start moving like him. Since Stokowski had such a distinct way of moving his hands, it created a distinct sound. His was an extreme case like that.

The same was true of Toscanini, but in a very different way. People who have listened to Toscanini could often recognize a recording as his by the sound itself. As a matter of fact, there was a funny anecdote that happened to me with Stokowski. When he first wanted to hire the Camerata Singers, it was for the *St. Matthew Passion* by J.S. Bach. It was quite fascinating. He called me to a meeting at his Fifth Avenue apartment, and tried to explain to me why the changes he was going to make were ones that Bach would have also made, had he been there that day. Some musicians we admire for doing things exactly as in the score, but Stokowski felt that you could make adjustments, because the environment and instruments were not the same ones now as the ones used back then. First, I had a rehearsal with the chorus alone, and then before his rehearsal, I took a half hour again with the chorus. I forgot at the time that he conducted without a baton, and I used a baton to prepare them during the rehearsal. He came walking up, and I put the baton down on the stand and said, "Maestro, please." He stood and looked at the music stand and saw the baton that I had left there. He picked it up with two fingers, looked at it with disgust, and dropped it on the floor. It was almost his trademark. At the end I offered to take him home to his apartment. He graciously accepted. My wife was in the car and I acted something like a chauffeur. I dropped him at his apartment that evening, Fifth Avenue beautifully lit in the night. He got out of the car, and while we were still inside, he took out of the lapel pocket of his jacket a silk handkerchief and waved to us. We drove away slowly, laughing so hard at how cute this man was—every bit the aristocrat!

I mean aristocrat in the best sense of the word. His music too, was PURE sound with a polish. Years later I analyzed how he produced it, and when I was working on the final section of the Fauré Requiem, *In paradisum*, I needed that sound, so I tried to emulate the way that he conducted—a little angular, like Stravinsky, but slow. It gave the music a stationary sheen, heavenly, but not alive—sexless, but angelically beautiful.

When Stravinsky got up and conducted the *Symphony of Psalms*, it was the same experience for me. The personality and characteristic of his conducting lent itself best to his own music, which is very angular. His conducting followed suit. Since the players and singers moved in order to be with him, they produced a sound that was appropriate and musical for that piece.

Students of conducting *should* watch others, and try to figure out what conductors are specifically doing to evoke certain sounds from an orchestra. General audiences often make the mistake that when they go to different conductor's performances they are going to hear different "interpretations" by those conductors. They think that the musical interpretation is an intellectual decision. But the interpretation is usually what comes from within the conductor and the way that he moves. A good conductor gets a performance that is individualistic to him, based not only on what he says and how he leads, but on how he moves and what he does.

– 11 –

ALFRED WALLENSTEIN

Overall, Wallenstein wasn't a pleasant fellow...but I remember one thing that was funny about him. As an objective observer, you might not find it as funny, so bear with me.

I was asked to prepare the Juilliard Chorus for him to conduct with the New York Philharmonic, a composition by Hector Berlioz, called *Romeo and Juliet*. It is of course a concert piece—but it follows the storyline of Romeo and Juliet. At one point in the music there is a garden scene where people are celebrating. This is depicted by the chorus, which is singing backstage. However, anyone who has been backstage in Carnegie Hall knows that for all practical purposes, there *is* no backstage (no room for a chorus, that is).

So we decided on the second best thing that we could do. Alongside the auditorium there are long corridors, where sometimes the audience goes out at intermission. That is where we chose to put the chorus.

Berlioz was a very smart man—he indicated in the score that the choral conductor should conduct the chorus backstage, and the orchestra conductor, who is on stage, should follow the choral sound. This is because the orchestra had very few notes to play, and they were mostly long sustained notes. Basically, the orchestra is just an accompanist to the chorus.

I was too young at the time to point out to Wallenstein what the score said. I'm sure he knew it, but he wanted somehow to be the conductor for the chorus—that is, I should conduct the chorus, but follow *his* conducting.

So what happened in rehearsals was already a bit bizarre, because by the time the sound got to him, we sounded as if we were late. He kept saying, "You're late, you're late." I said, "Maestro, I think we are with you, but by the time the sound gets to you, it sounds like we're late." He says to me, "Anticipate!" OK, so I said to myself, I will not wait—I will conduct a bit earlier than him, and he will think that we are with him.

What we didn't anticipate was that this was a February night, and it was one of the coldest nights in Manhattan. And I had to open the door to the auditorium in order to listen to the orchestra, which was playing very, very softly in anticipation of the choral entry, and then give the chorus the starting pitch and bring them in. The whole thing was quite tricky. We didn't anticipate such cold weather that night, and we were freezing in there. That corridor insulated the auditorium from the weather outside, so the minute I opened the door in order to hear what the orchestra was playing, the entire audience on our side turned around to us because a cold breeze rushed through the door. So the first whispers were, "Close the door!"

I said, "I can't, we have to sing from backstage." That happened quite a few times, repeating itself in the first and later performances. I kept repeating the scenario and discussion with different members of the audience. The last time that it happened, somebody from the audience asked, "Why?" and I said, "Because they won't let us in!"

In a little book of anecdotes about conductors, I was reminded of another story about Wallenstein. Wallenstein was the first cellist in the New York Philharmonic when Toscanini was the music director. He adored Toscanini so much that no other conductor existed or meant anything to him. One day, Bruno Walter came as a guest conductor. He noticed that this young cellist was playing, and his face was turned away from the conductor—as if to make certain that Walter would know that he wasn't watching him.

Walter, being a gentle man, asked the general manager to request of the first cellist to come and see him in the green room (this was during a rehearsal). Unsuspecting, because this was not an unusual request, Wallenstein came to the room to greet Walter. Walter asked, "Young man, what is your ambition in life? Are you happy with being the first cellist?" He said "No, I want to be a conductor." Walter said, "I wish you the best of luck—and I wish that you will have an Alfred Wallenstein as a first cellist." I suspect that Wallenstein didn't get the joke.

– 12 –

RAFAEL KUBELIK

Kubelik was a world-renowned conductor when I met him, and before the new General Manager of the Metropolitan Opera was killed in a traffic accident in Italy with his entire family, he appointed Rafael Kubelik to be the new Music Director at the Met. Kubelik was a talented conductor, particularly gifted at conducting Western European music, because of his special love for this repertoire.

I had the great privilege of working with him when he guest conducted the New York Philharmonic. He chose the *Stabat Mater* by Dvorak. As would happen very often, the conductor who came to guest conduct would ask me to have one run-through with the chorus in a piano rehearsal with him. Then, we would of course join the orchestra.

As I was conducting for him, I could see him from the corner of my eye. I was delighted to see that the man was beaming, relishing in the music—he could not wipe the smile off his face. That was what most struck me about Kubelik, evident throughout the rest of his time with the Philharmonic. Every note that he conducted both in rehearsals and in the performance was filled with pure rapture for his love of music. So when I think of Rafael Kubelik, I think of a talented soul, thoroughly transformed and smitten by music.

− 13 −

DARIUS MILHAUD

Darius Milhaud became something of a father figure to me in Israel when I was twenty-three. At that time I dared to ask him if what Time Magazine wrote about him was correct. The publication reported that Milhaud was commissioned to write the Opera *Columbus* by the Italian Government, and the audience threw tomatoes at the first performance. While I was asking him whether the story was true, a big smile crossed his face and he said, "Yes, yes, it did happen." I asked why he was smiling—he responded, "Can you imagine how I would have felt if they fell asleep?"

We asked Milhaud at a seminar in Aspen how he pronounced his name. He said, "Our family is named after a little town in France—everyone in France called it Millo—we, in the town, called it 'Miyo.'"

One of the students of composition in the class in Aspen brought a piece that didn't seem to make any musical sense to Darius Milhaud. Milhaud became very upset, and actually began to verbally attack the student for a few minutes. He sat down at the piano, and tried to play a few bars of the string quartet. As he was trying to play the music, he asked, "Why does this violin have an F sharp, and in the Viola part a G flat? Obviously, you don't hear it (what you're writing)." Then Milhaud felt terrible about his actions—here was a young man who came to study with him as master. Attempting to alleviate the tension he had created, he asked what the man did. He said, "I teach harmony class at a college." Milhaud, unable to control himself, whispered under his breath, "Those who don't know, teach". Well, then he REALLY felt terrible!

The reason the music came out in one voice as F sharp and the other G flat is because it was part of a tone row. In the second half of the twentieth century there was a new form of composition called twelve-tone technique, initiated by Schoenberg. Instead of using the traditional scales in music, he treated all of the half steps of the octave equally. The idea was to give all half steps equal importance. In order to organize the music, you start writing a tone row. Choose any notes. Then, you take them through the ringer—write them backwards, in mirror fashion, etc... This is supposed to give unity to the composition, in an non-traditional way. When Schoenberg wrote many of his compositions they were called "atonal," and in many people's opinion the twelve-tone system was invented to take away the negative connotation of "atonal."

So the young man explained, "It is written in twelve-tone—that is why when I write it from this side, it is like F sharp, and that side is G flat." Milhaud didn't want to criticize him anymore, so he instead started reminiscing: "You know... I used to hate to go to England. Every time I traveled there, an old woman used to trap me at the airport and tell me everything that she was struggling with in composition. As I departed the airplane, I dreaded the meeting. One time, she was waving and waving, but she was so happy. I wondered what it was. When we met, she said, 'Oh, Mr. Milhaud, I am so happy!' "I said, 'Aren't you still struggling with composition?' She said, 'Oh no—now I am writing twelve-tone, and I can write every day.'"

We all laughed a bit. He was living at that time in California, where Schoenberg was also living. He told another story: "One day, when I came back from France, I saw my friend, Schoenberg—I said, 'Mr.

Schoenberg, you should be very happy—I just returned from Europe, and there is a whole generation of young people that are starting to compose in your twelve-tone system.' Schoenberg asked, 'Tell me, are they putting any music into it?'"

My personal opinion? Notes are very much like speech—you can say a lot of words and say nothing.

As for his own composition, it is understandably very French. Even in the instrumental music, you can somehow hear the French language. One episode during my studies with him in Aspen was very revealing, both in terms of his positive attitude and in terms of something that he was often criticized for. During his lifetime—and I guess it is valid from a certain point of view—some musicians criticized Milhaud for writing too much music. They implied that it was careless, and that most of it was mediocre, with very few outstanding pieces. On the other hand, when he was confronted by that question, he gave an answer that to me was very French. The answer was simply that if you are a composer, you write. He told that to one of his composition classes that I attended. Some students entered the class with the assumption that they should only compose when "inspired." He reframed the idea by saying that if one is a composer, he writes. I personally can't make a judgment as to whether that is a good or bad idea—but it is very French. I had heard similar words of discipline from William Schuman, but from Milhaud the same words had a sense of lightness—encouraging students not to take themselves so seriously. We know, for instance, that Beethoven would write and rewrite pieces sometimes for twenty-five years before he would finish. On the other hand, Mozart wrote very fast. So what are the critics of Darius Milhaud saying? That he is not as talented as Mozart? What Milhaud himself is saying is something along the lines of, "I know I'm not as talented as Mozart, but as a composer, I still have to write. I cannot sit and agonize over whether I was inspired enough."

— 14 —

GEORGE SZELL

I was asked to prepare Beethoven's *Symphony No. 9* right after Szell became the chief guest conductor of the New York Philharmonic (the year after Bernstein). I think he was technically the "interim music director" or something like that.

He also was advisor to the board of the symphony, because it eventually appointed Pierre Boulez based upon his recommendation. I believe it was that year (because he was appointed guest music director of the New York Philharmonic along with his directorship of the Cleveland Symphony) that he was chosen by *Musical America* as Musician of the Year, or by *Time* magazine as Man of the Year, and even appeared on the cover. While the players were scared of him, he knew how to flatter members of the board.

At the time, I didn't know anything about his reputation. We had eighty to a hundred members of the Camerata singers, and they knew the piece we were to sing very well. We didn't need much rehearsal. I had one two-hour rehearsal—the first hour by myself, the second with Szell. Although the *Ninth Symphony* is difficult on the voice, there are only ten to fifteen minutes of singing in it. For the singers who had sung it before, more rehearsal was not necessary.

Szell began rehearsing with the chorus members, and started to do a very strange thing. He corrected their German diction in places where they didn't make any mistakes, saying "Don't say it like that, say it like this." I'd seen many choral conductors do this kind of nonsense just to show off, but I had never seen an orchestral conductor do it - especially one who was not German himself! It was obvious that something was not going well. When the choral rehearsal was over, he did not say anything, and we entered the joint rehearsal with orchestra. Immediately after the rehearsal, he called me to his dressing room. He asked me, "How many hours did you rehearse with the chorus?" When I began to tell him, he said "Yes, I knew it! They need to be together longer to feel it." I asked, "Maestro, what did they do wrong?" He again repeated, "They aren't feeling it." After every rehearsal he complained. In one encounter he said, "You know the difficult section in the chorus? Nobody prepares this well except for Robert Shaw!" I said, "Well, we all know there is only one Robert Shaw." Szell looked like someone had tossed ice water in his face, because I was objective enough not to be insulted.

Typically, conductors tell us that they want us backstage so that they can bring us on stage to give us an honorary bow after the piece. When our performance time came, Szell acted as if he was so angry at me, that I just figured I wouldn't even go backstage after the first performance. This made him even more furious, and he asked why I wasn't there. So for the next performance I *did* wait there, and he ignored me. I said to my wife, "If I never work for this S.O.B. again, I will not miss it for a moment." To my surprise, the next morning one of the New York Philharmonic officials called me to say "Maestro Szell *agreed* that you should prepare Brahms' *German Requiem* for next year." He didn't live to conduct it the following year, and instead, Robert Shaw conducted the piece as his memorial.

Walter Gould* published the compositions of many musicians, and

---

* Brother of composer Morton Gould.

actually started the publishing company Lawson/Gould with Robert Shaw. Lawson was Shaw's middle name. When I saw him the next time, I told him the story about how Szell behaved, and he said, "Oh, he does that all the time. George would humiliate Robert every once in a while, and Shaw would walk out and say he was never coming back. But then Szell would go to his apartment, say, 'There, there, I didn't mean it,' and Shaw would come back."

There is no doubt that George Szell was one of the world class conductors of our age—but in my own experience working with him, I barely sensed the joy of music in him. It seemed that his actions were more motivated by the exercise of his power as a conductor. I write this at the risk of appearing too harsh—as I am trying to remain transparent throughout this volume, and hope that my comments are taken in context. Perhaps this chapter should have appeared in the "What Might Have Been Splendid Encounters" version of the book!

– 15 –

SKITCH HENDERSON

Skitch Henderson was the band leader under Johnny Carson for the Tonight show. When the New York Philharmonic decided to celebrate the twenty-fifth anniversary of *Oklahoma* (the musical) by Richard Rodgers, the organization thought it would be appropriate to invite someone from the pop field to conduct the performance. Unfortunately for Skitch, the exercise became a wonderful illustration of how a pop music leader is not necessarily qualified to conduct a symphony orchestra. He had great difficulty making transitions from one piece to another in a way that the musicians could understand, simply because he had never developed a conducting technique that applied to a symphony orchestra.

The orchestra came to the rehearsal and the music just fell apart. Richard Rodgers was fuming. Of course, they figured it out eventually, and it was wonderful. One of the reasons that the New York Philharmonic thought to celebrate *Oklahoma* was that it was the first of what became a standard format for American musicals. England had Gilbert & Sullivan, who wrote stage shows that were similar to the American musical. Europe had operettas. All three shared the idea that they were not operas, in the sense that not every word was sung. Basically, it was the spoken word interrupted by music.

Anyhow, I was just there, desperate to help him if he would ask,

63

but there was nothing that I could do…and so he struggled. He had never conducted something that moved from one number into the next with various transitions, and had never needed the discipline of conducting in particular patterns, which a symphonic conductor *must* do. He had never learned to slow down an entire orchestra from tempo to tempo. Nevertheless, he was a great musician and eventually, it was a wonderful, wonderful performance.

Henderson was a very nice fellow. We really didn't have too much to talk about, though, because he was so busy at that time—and he used every moment of his time with us to survive musically. In addition, he had to learn orchestral conducting while watching Rodgers become more and more frustrated on the sidelines.

I guess the situation was the reverse of my own experience conducting for Frank Sinatra—and at the time, I asked for as much help as I could! But to Henderson's credit, it is always easier to go from classical to popular music on a technical level, than the other way around.

In terms of temperament, Skitch Henderson was the right person for the piece. In many ways, I was aching for him and for Rodgers; for him, because he found himself in an embarrassing situation, and for Rodgers, because it was such a huge event. He had obviously never had his pieces played by the New York Philharmonic—what an opportunity! But when the performance came, everything was straightened out, and the audience had a marvelous time, including myself. There were many great musicians, and Henderson figured out what he had to do for that piece. The soloists knew their parts inside and out, and there was a great spirit to the performance. In addition, the musicians in the orchestra knew how to adjust, because not all symphonic conductors have the same caliber of technical skills. Some are easy to play for, and some are hard to follow. So they are used to adjusting, and if given the time, can usually play well.

I recall a joke which illustrates the point of how American orchestras, by and large, in the last fifty years have tried to help their guest conductors. There is a story about one of the old fashioned conductors who thought that being a good conductor meant that you yelled at the orchestra. In that vein, he kept yelling at the orchestra until finally they got tired of him. One member raised his hand and said in frustration, "Maestro, if you keep carrying on like this, we are going to play *exactly* as you are conducting!"

All right, another yelling conductor joke: A conductor was yelling at the orchestra and at one point went off the deep end. He said, "I don't know what's the matter with you—I've taught you everything I know…and you know nothing!"

I digress. The point about the performance is that Skitch was an excellent band director in his capacity for the Tonight Show. In this case, he was out of his element, but after a lot of hard work and adjustment by the musicians, his overall temperament allowed the piece to come through.

− 16 −

THOMAS SCHIPPERS

Internationally known as a conductor, Thomas Schippers began as an organist, later became an opera conductor, and eventually became an orchestral conductor. Because of his experience with the opera, he wound up being one of the best conductors when it came to conducting chorus and orchestra together. He had a feel for the chorus second only to Bernstein, in my opinion. Once when he guest conducted with the New York Philharmonic, Bernstein suggested to him that he use another chorus instead of my professional chorus, the Camerata Singers, maybe to spread the work around, and Schippers responded, "*You* use another chorus!" He laughed because he assumed that Bernstein would never do that—and he figured I would be amused. He had strong feelings about it.

He conducted a lot in the Menotti Festival, which was done in Italy (Spoleto Festival). As a matter of fact, I believe there was a version of the Spoleto Festival in this country. I prepared choruses for him three times. The first time was when he conducted the Rossini *Stabat Mater,* which became a favorite of mine. Once it was for an obscure cantata by Beethoven, *Cantata on the Death of Emperor Joseph II.*

There is a funny story about that Beethoven cantata. The piece was written for the funeral of the Emperor. Schippers had dug it up and performed it in Germany. The cantata starts with the orchestra, and the chorus comes in with a low, often-repeated "Tod" (death). The Germans, as reserved as they are, all started laughing because the chorus just kept repeating the word. When Schippers brought the cantata to the United States to perform, I realized it was in Latin. I asked him why it was in Latin. "Did Beethoven write it in Latin?" "No," he replied, "I did it in Europe in German, and the crowd started laughing." So to avoid this happening again, he translated the piece into Latin for the chorus, which changed the word "Tod" into "Morse."

He was wonderful with the chorus. The chorus senses if the conductor breathes with them, and phrases with them—very much like an orchestra can tell when a conductor is comfortable. A conductor really gets what he wants by the way he moves. Schippers' movements were very elegant; therefore the music shared that quality of sound.

Schippers was very, very friendly, and he used to dress in a very spiffy fashion. He always seemed to wear a suit, but even his casual clothes were kind of special. He was also aware of the fact that he was quite handsome, and this too was part of his demeanor.

Although he was born in this country, he had an unusually strong affinity for Italian music. For an American-born conductor, to have such identification with the Italian temperament was quite remarkable, and it clearly came through in his music making.

− 17 −

NEVILLE MARRINER

Marriner is probably the most recorded conductor of classical music to date. I worked with him once when Daniel Barenboim was first scheduled to conduct the New York Philharmonic in a minor Mozart choral piece. For some reason or another, Barenboim cancelled, and Neville Marriner replaced him.

I discovered something about Marriner and choral conducting which was delightful. I don't know if it was his own characteristic, or because he was a part of the English tradition. There is a great choral tradition in England—there are many community choruses, one in almost every town.

The detail that impressed me the most requires a little bit of background explanation: In this country, we routinely place final consonants on the following rests. A final consonant is the one that appears on the last word before the musical line has a rest. For instance, in the choral movement, *He Watching Over Israel Slumbers not nor Sleeps,* we have two consonants, 'p' and 's' at the end of the word "sleeps." When this phrase is finished by one voice, another voice takes over. This comes from Mendelssohn's *Elijah,* by the way. As I have said, in this country the *modus operandi* of our choruses is to place the final consonant, or double consonant in this case, on the following musical rest. So if for example in the first statement above, the last note is a whole note, we place the final consonant on the *next* downbeat, which is the rest. But the problem with this arrangement, especially in this example, is that the next voice starts on that same downbeat. While one voice is saying "ps," the other voice is starting, "He." In this particular case of course, most conductors realize that the overlap doesn't make sense, so they shorten the sustained whole note and put the "ps" on the fourth beat of the whole note so that the downbeat of the next measure remains absolutely clear, to make room for the next voice to begin cleanly. The other problem that we have in America with this practice of putting the consonant on the following rest is that if the consonant happens to be what we call a "voiced" consonant, like a "b" or a "d", as in the word "God," the last consonant will have a pitch. In order to be heard in the music, we have to add an unwritten vowel behind the sound 'd'. If the chord under the next downbeat is different from the chord under the whole note, you will get the pitch from the previous chord sounding on top of the new chord.

So this is the problem that we face in this country with our way of doing things. The revelation that I had, when I met Marriner before the concert to ask how he wanted it to be prepared, was that I was pleasantly surprised to find that he clearly wanted the final consonant to be sung on the fourth beat of the whole note. I don't know if this is British tradition, or if it was Marriner's own genius. In this country I, myself, always place the final consonants within the final beat, rather than in the next rest. As a matter of fact the few times that I do place it on the following rest are really the exception.

One of the reasons these problems exist with us is that until thirty years ago, composers never worried about diction, and didn't bother to clarify these details. So now, when we add refinement to choral music by adding elements of diction that make the words easier to understand, or that will make the phrases go together, we should do it in a way that will enhance the piece, rather than superimpose on it and distract from the piece.

For example, if an audience comes out of a concert and says, "Wow, what great diction they had!" You might ask the audience what the chorus sang about, and if they don't remember, this defeats the purpose. The only purpose of good diction is to understand what the text is about.

When Marriner answered my question, "Always within the length of the final note" (before the rest), I appreciated that he had thought about this and come to the same conclusion…no other conductor ever pointed that out to me, either before or since. Most orchestral conductors will just say, "Do whatever you think is right."

Neville Marriner's conducting style is very clean and professional. He doesn't try to add his own personality to what is already excellently written. Being an objective choral professional, I think he is doing a great job. The closest thing to him in terms of style is Pierre Boulez.

Many years ago there were people who said that Hermann Scherchen, a very famous conductor, was the greatest interpreter of Bach's choral works. When someone asked Stravinsky if he agreed with this, he said in his inimitable style, "No, I think he is the worst performer of Bach." When asked, "Why do you say so?" He replied "Because he *does* things to Bach—and Bach doesn't need anything done to him."

At the end of the twentieth century, it was very fashionable to take Bach's music and put your own interpretation on it, but as years went by, the more we went back to the original, the more we realized that Bach sounded best exactly as written.

– 18 –

JOSEF KRIPS

I met Josef Krips when he was scheduled to conduct the Bruckner Mass in F Minor with the New York Philharmonic. I'd gotten a message through the Philharmonic that he wanted to perform it in accordance with a tradition in Vienna, where he was born. Since the Gloria and the Credo of the mass are both in C major, the tradition is that between these two movements an unaccompanied motet by Bruckner, also in C major, is performed.

He asked that we prepare the *Ave Maria* motet by Bruckner. I was looking forward to the experience greatly for the simple reason that to that point, I had never warmed up to the music of Bruckner, especially to the large pieces, although I loved some of the motets. The masses—I just thought they were OK. I was sure that it was my fault and not Bruckner's, because when you have a whole audience, even when it is concentrated in one area like Austria, that *loves* Bruckner so much, you've got to figure he's just one of the great composers that doesn't seem to speak to me (Don't compare him to Wagner—his fans were more of a cult, but that is another story.)

So, here I thought I would have the chance to work with a conductor that might have the "inside scoop" on what the music was supposed to do. The big surprise for me was that before he even arrived, I suddenly discovered Bruckner for myself.

What had bothered me before about Bruckner was that there were modulations to different keys at different times that didn't seem to make any sense. It seemed to be capricious, something he did just to be different. I would move along, enjoying the music up to a point, and would suddenly hit a turn that didn't make any sense.

So as I always did when preparing for other conductors, I tried to follow the score to the letter, implementing every dynamic marking, tempo, and other detail noted in the manuscript. Suddenly, at one of the rehearsals, I realized that the piece made absolute sense from the first note to the last. It finally registered for me. So I looked back and tried to analyze what happened. Why was it not satisfactory to me before, and now it was? My discovery was that it had nothing to do with "getting used to it." What I had been doing (wrong) before when studying Bruckner, was that I was listening to the melodic phrases as second-rate Beethoven. I would conduct the melody, and expect it to develop and emerge like a Beethoven melody. So for a Beethoven melody, the sudden turns didn't make any sense. But now that I had observed the dynamics exactly as I saw them on the page, I suddenly realized that I was able to listen to it or hear it or conduct it like a first-rate Bruckner melody, not a second-rate Beethoven melody.

For example, the first theme of the *Kyrie eleison* from Bruckner's F Minor Mass actually starts on its highest point, and then the rest of it trails downward. This is very different from other composer's *kyrie eleisons*. In the Schubert *Mass in G Major*, the *kyrie eleison* starts with a scale going up. The same happens in Beethoven's Mass in *C Major*—it starts with a scale going up. The F Minor Mass by Bruckner on the other hand, starts with the scale coming down. In both Schubert and Beethoven, the phrase leads to kyrie el-**EI**-son (Lord have **MERCY**). The Bruckner theme, on the other hand, starts **KY**-rie eleison. This showed me how a person could learn all of the notes and still not understand all of the music.

Anyhow, by the time the rehearsal came along with Krips, I already knew how to conduct the piece. When the chorus sang the *Ave Maria* between the Gloria and the Credo, Krips made a mistake that many conductors do—both orchestral and choral. The moment that he came to that point in the piano rehearsal, he gave the chorus a little speech. He said to them, I want you to know that all choruses go flat on these long a capella pieces—so I want you to do the following: keep pitching the piece a little bit up. It was crucial that we start in C major from the Gloria and end in C major for the entry into the Credo.

Well, I have a whole chapter in my *Choral Conducting* book about this subject (something that I have learned about intonation in vocal music). Most of the time as a result, a speech such as the one that Krips gave would turn into a self-fulfilling prophecy. As predicted in this situation…that is exactly what happened. The amazing thing is that the chorus *never* went flat in rehearsals, where they were spared the speech.

I had some experience with this as a singer in a professional chorus in Israel, with many refugee singers from Austria and Germany, who could read music quite well in comparison to the Israeli singers. Conductors came and pushed and pushed us in the same way. For example, we had to record a short, rhythmic, thirty-two-bar marching song, with which it should have been easy to stay in tune, because it was a reasonably fast tempo. All of the corrections, however made matters worse! We ended up recruiting a string quartet to sit in the middle of us, and we *still* went flat. It made a big impression on me from that time on that this was not the thing to say or do—it only makes things worse.

Krips came to me and asked, "Do you have any suggestions?" I said, "Maestro, do me a big, big favor. I have developed some subtle ways of keeping a chorus from going flat. I will take them by myself for thirty minutes and rehearse with them. When you come to take over, conduct them as if they were an orchestra, and don't say anything to them about pushing the pitch up or anything." And so it was, the chorus performed perfectly.

The reason that a chorus goes flat—the main reason—on a long sustained piece of choral music, is because it sings without breath support. For example, before you sing a phrase, you inhale some air. When you sing, it goes through the vocal chords and produces sound. If you go into a long sustained melody and don't prepare with enough breath, your voice will trail down toward the end. In our culture everyone equates going flat with not being musical.

In general, whenever I met people that immediately told me that they couldn't even carry a tune, I didn't believe them. The fact is that singing flat has nothing to do with how musical a person is—it has everything to do with not having proper vocal support and breath control. When you *tell* a singer, as Krips did, that they are always going to sing flat, they get nervous and/or insulted. This is the guarantee that they will not breathe correctly—hence, the self-fulfilling prophecy.

I am especially grateful to Krips that by preparing for this mass, I discovered Bruckner for the first time. It is a lesson that I now apply to other composers. Now, whenever I don't warm up to or understand a particular composer, I question myself as to whether I am trying to compare him or her to another composer who might seem similar. The trick to letting a composer's music reach you is to stop seeing him or her as a second-rate version of somebody else, and to start seeing him as a first-rate version of himself.

– 19 –

MARIAN ANDERSON & FRANK MILLER

Marian Anderson was a superb alto, who broke the color barrier by being the first African American woman to sing at the Metropolitan Opera.

At one point William Steinberg invited me to share the conducting duties in a concert of the Israeli Philharmonic and the NBC Symphony by conducting a piece by Robert Starer. The two orchestras came together for this concert in Carnegie Hall on Toscanini's hundredth birthday, because the America Israel Foundation decided to do its annual concert in his memory. William Steinberg was asked to conduct the concert. The reason that they combined the two orchestras was that the NBC Symphony had been Toscanini's orchestra, and the Israeli Philharmonic (the Palestine Philharmonic, at the time) was inaugurated by Toscanini.

Steinberg decided at the time to include a new work in the program by Robert Starer, which was a choral work entitled *Joseph and his Brethren*. The connection with Robert Starer, besides the fact that Steinberg loved his music, was that Starer had spent many of his young years in Israel, so Steinberg thought it would be appropriate. Then he decided that I should be the one to conduct that particular work in the concert. Of course, this was one of the greatest experiences of my life, because there I was standing in front of an incredible orchestra containing two famous concertmasters sitting side by side: the famed Misha Mishakov from the NBC Symphony, and Zvi Haftel of the Israeli Philharmonic. In the viola section the first violist was William Primrose (the only violist who toured as a soloist at that time), and the first cellist was Frank Miller, who was already the first cellist of the Chicago Symphony.

I had only one rehearsal for this performance, and as I said, it was one of the greatest experiences of my musical life. Primrose, who was quite old at the time, had a hearing aid and could barely see, came to me after the rehearsal and said "Young man, I have been playing in orchestras for many years. If I can follow you, you must be OK." It was a very big compliment because the musicians were all drawn away from some of the best orchestras to play for the NBC Symphony, and once Toscanini went away, most of them did not want to go back to any other orchestras. For that concert, all of the retired players who had left came back just for the tribute.

Although the piece was not written with a narrator in mind, someone decided, to my good fortune, to ask Marian Anderson to narrate the story in between movements.

She was an amazing person. In spite of going through many humiliating, racially prejudiced experiences in her youth, she managed to keep a great sense of dignity about her. Later in life she was appointed as U.S. delegate to the United Nations. In the name of the UN, she toured overseas; One of the foreign journalists asked her, "How do you feel about people in your country who put you down just because of your color?" She replied, "I feel sorry for them, because when a person has to work so hard to keep people down, that person is probably very down themselves." She didn't have any animosity, despite her hard life, and always kept her dignity about her. That is why this particular concert was such an experience for me—besides having the opportunity to conduct such great musicians, I was able to share a stage with this amazing woman as she narrated the story.

During rehearsals I was very careful, trying not to give the musicians too many instructions, as they were so experienced. I knew that all I had to do was conduct well, and I would get results. As you can imagine, I studied the score very well and proceeded to run through it during rehearsal. At one point, there was a very short solo for the first cellist. Since musically, it was not a very important part of the piece at the time, I didn't even look at him (it is a sign of an amateur conductor to stare at the soloist when it is his turn).

That cellist played his little solo *so musically*, that it *made* it more important. For a moment I had to turn and look at him, as if to say, "Who is this man?" There he was, a very big man, very calmly playing his instrument in the only way that he knew, absolutely full of musicality. The cellist was Frank Miller.

Many years later, when I went to congratulate James DePreist (Director of Conducting and Orchestral Studies, Laureate Music Director of the Oregon Symphony and Marian Anderson's nephew) after a concert of the Juilliard orchestra in San Diego, I related the story to him and his wife. When I expressed my surprise and gratitude that Marian Anderson had accepted the role of narrator, Mrs. DePreist said, "Don't you realize, it was Toscanini who broke the color barrier and hired her to sing with the Metropolitan Opera."

– 20 –

ZOLTÁN KODÁLY

Zoltán Kodály was an outstanding Hungarian composer who started his activities jointly with Bella Bartok. They were known to have embarked many, many years ago on a project of collecting Hungarian folk songs.

I had the great pleasure of meeting Zoltán Kodály under charming and strange circumstances. At the time, I was taping a performance for CBS Television of his *Missa Brevis* (short mass, in Latin). It was a composition that he wrote during World War II, and which was first performed in the basement of the Hungarian Opera House while the German armies were surrounding Budapest. It was written before Hungary became a communist satellite of the Soviet Union, and was really a religious piece. Since most of the musicians were stuck in the basement of the Opera House, the first performance occurred with all of the singers of the opera company singing the chorus parts, and some of the solo parts. It was written originally for organ and chorus.

I knew it when I was a student in Israel, and I had already fallen in love with it. I thought it was one of the most moving pieces written in the twentieth century. So when I was preparing for that performance, we heard that Kodály was in the United States. Years later he had become a high official in the Hungarian government (Minister of Education, I believe). In fact, he was so popular in his country that

I believe the Hungarians wanted to elect him as president. As part of his job, or perhaps because he was very interested in education, he devised a special system for sight-singing which was very appropriate and helpful for young children in school. It was later dubbed the Kodály Method.

We heard that he was invited to the United States to lecture during that time period about the Kodály Method. It used hand signals and other kinds of interesting things that appealed to young children very much.

My friend (and CBS Television Producer) at the time, Pamela Illot, said to me, "why don't we go and try to convince him to come and listen to his *Missa brevis*? Maybe he'll let us interview him too." We found him and the first thing that he said was an emphatic NO. He said it was because American TV was the epitome of capitalism, and we would exploit him. He didn't speak English, but had a young wife who spoke English quite well. We explained to her that we didn't want to exploit him—we just wanted him to come and listen. If he had remarks about the performance, then we might film him—we just wanted the composer there to tell us if we were performing it right.

Eventually he believed us and agreed to come. We arrived to perform at Riverside Church in New York, which had great acoustics. When I thought of the first performance in the basement in Hungary, which used two harmoniums (they didn't have an organ), by comparison I think that performance when the church was quite empty, the acoustics must have been quite stunning to him.

Anyhow, he sat with quite a severe face. I got up, and conducted the whole thing from memory, because I knew the piece so well and loved it.

Very gingerly I went to where he was sitting and asked him, "Maestro, is everything OK?" Very angrily, he said to me "Where did you get that version!? I thought that Boosey & Hawkes had pulled that old version off the market because I have a new version of the piece." So I said, "Maestro, they did pull the old version off the market. But I must make a confession—I've known that version since a few years after you wrote it, and I loved it so much, I had the chorus make the changes back to the original version in pencil. If you say so, the members of the chorus are professionals and within five minutes, can return to the new version. That's why we wanted you here."

So he sat and thought about it—"Well…no, leave it this way, it is really wonderful"

I learned several things from that encounter, including how to perform that particular piece. The reason he made those changes, I believe, was because the nationalism at the time caused him to want to release a piece with a huge orchestra, a mighty sound. The changes were made to accommodate the large orchestration.

As I've learned from trying to improve upon my own old compositions, very often my original hunches were better.

Also, when I listened to the orchestrated recording before I met him, I realized that he was not a skilled conductor. There were markings in the score that implied faster or slower tempos. This would have required a conductor with good technical skill. The transitions in the recording were not very good and were sometimes even opposed to what was in the score.

Anyhow, after that I asked him several questions, including the following: "First, in the original version you have a prologue with the organ, which in church usually provides improvisational music while the congregation is coming in. Then, after the entire text of the mass is sung, the organist plays an epilogue, which you titled *Ite missa est* (translated 'Thus ends the mass'). This again provides musical improvisation while the congregation leaves, in the musical theme of the mass . But then in the new one, you took the *Ite missa est*, and you superimposed choral lines with the two words, "da pacem" (of peace). Why did you add the voices?" He said, "Well, I've attended so many performances of it, and the organist took such freedoms with the music that I couldn't recognize what I wrote. So I decided that I would add voices so that somebody would have to conduct it, and then I would recognize the piece. Not only that—but if you're not performing in church, you don't even need the *Ite missa est*—leave it out!" I never would have dared to do that myself, but it made sense.

In a word, I think of Kodály as being the quintessential Hungarian composer. What it means is that if you had been exposed to the folk songs of the Hungarian culture, you would have no doubt that his is Hungarian music. While Bartok has those influences as well, Bartok's music also contains various other international influences. Kodály's is more purely Hungarian at its core.

– 21 –

GERARD SCHWARZ

I was conducting my first performance of Bach's *B minor Mass* in Carnegie Hall. The concert was sold out weeks ahead of time, and it took place sometime in February. That day, the snow started coming down, and there was something like two to three feet of snow. Everything in the city stopped—the subways weren't running, nothing. Some of the streets were cleared, but still it was dismal.

The time for the concert came, and miraculously, most of the orchestra made it through the snow. As the time came closer, all but one player, an oboeist, arrived. The missing musician kept calling Carnegie Hall from different parts of Brooklyn saying that he was trying to get there. He took the subway to different stations, but kept getting stuck.

We kept postponing the beginning of the concert to wait for him, because he was also playing the oboe d'amore. I was sitting in the Green Room, and didn't really know what to do. We looked at the audience, and even though we knew it was sold out (around three thousand seats in the hall), there were only about a hundred and fifty people seated there so far. We had the entire orchestra (minus one) and almost the entire chorus.

So we sat there and the orchestra contractor came to me, bringing a young trumpet player who couldn't have been more than seventeen years old. I had heard of Gerard Schwarz because he was so appreciated by his Juilliard teacher that he was often brought as an assistant to the New York Philharmonic rehearsals (his teacher was the first-trumpet player for the Philharmonic). Anyhow, this man brought in Gerry Schwarz, and said to me "You know, Gerry says that he can play the oboe d'amore part *con sordino* (with a mute), which should make the trumpet sound a little bit like the oboe d'amore." I also realized that to do this he would have to transpose it (the trumpet is a B flat instrument.) So I said, thinking about it, "Gerry, thanks very much, but no thanks." This was my first performance of the *B minor Mass* at Carnegie Hall—I just couldn't do it. While we were talking, luckily the oboe player came in. We all ran back to the stage, I came out, and apologized to the audience. "I apologize for our rudeness in being late, but as you can see by looking around you, we miraculously had only one player who had difficulties getting here from Brooklyn, and he just showed up. We appreciate you all for fighting the elements to get here, and we will try to give you the best performance that we can, because you all deserve it."

Years later I found out that Schwarz had a very well rounded musical education, which explains why he went into conducting.

Another time, I was performing the *Messiah* at Avery Fischer Hall in New York and Schwarz was in the orchestra. At the end of the Amen chorus, he asked me if I would like him to improvise the cadence before the last chord of the work, which had been very customary to do. I said sure, by all means to let me hear it. At every run through he did a slightly different improvisation, and each one was beautiful, imaginative and musical. At the last rehearsal he asked me "Which one would you like me to do in the performance?" I told him, "Surprise me—do whatever sounds good to you at the moment, whatever fits." I had no doubt, because of how musical each improvisation was, that he would do something that worked perfectly.

– 22 –

ROBERT STARER

Robert Starer was probably one of the most talented all-around musicians that I ever met and was able to associate with for a long period of time. He was on the faculty before I came to Juilliard, and we developed a wonderful friendship. When I say he was one of the most talented, it is because he was an extremely gifted pianist, wonderful composer, and he had an ear that many conductors would envy, although he wasn't interested in conducting. As a result I had the benefit of premiering most of his choral works. I discovered that this was true, when I received a call one day from a lady who was pursuing a doctorate on his music at Brooklyn College. She said to me "You know, I'm preparing a doctorate on the music of Robert Starer, and he told me to interview you because you had premiered most of his choral works." That was the first time that I realized it.

He taught composition, and was a very prolific composer himself - but was by no means only a choral composer. He wrote several piano concertos, and he wrote for a great number of instruments. As a matter of fact, I was away when he wrote perhaps his best choral composition, *Ariel (Visions of Isaiah.)* That work was commissioned by a group called the "Interracial Chorus of New York," with a wonderful conductor by the name of Harold Ax. I think it was written between the years that I studied at Juilliard and the time I was in Israel before returning to the

U.S. (1958-1959). When I returned, Robert Starer gave me the score of Ariel. I spent all night studying it, and called him first thing in the morning, saying, "Robert, this will be your most performed choral piece ever. I am only sorry that I wasn't around to perform the premiere." I made up for it later by performing the first and only recording of the piece. One side of the album was Ariel, and one was "Concerto a Tres." Gerard Schwarz played the trumpet on that one.

I also had the pleasure of commissioning Starer to write five pieces for the Collegiate Chorale, which we premiered. I believe it was called, "Five Sayings." While he was in the process, one of the pieces that he wrote was called *A little Nonsense Now and Then is Relished by the Wisest Men*. In it, he made a very subtle joke about people who were writing twelve-tone music. When I saw and asked about it, I had to admit that I couldn't figure it out. He said, "See, I did the retrograde (a series of notes played through once and then repeated backward) in the text instead of in the music"—so I looked at it and the retrograde spelling was backwards, but you couldn't recognize it as backwards because the letters were nonsensical. I said to him, "Why not, instead of doing a retrograde of the letters, do the syllables? For example, in your text, first write "reli, reli, relish-ed," then "shedli, shedli, shedli-re." We collaborated on a few things like this.

I had another occasion with him that was very interesting. When I went to London and brought back my recording of *Glorious*, I was reminded of his marvelous ear. He sat and listened to the album for me, because it was the first time I'd written something. He said, "I noticed something very interesting—you never go above G for the sopranos." He decided that he could learn from me because I had so much experience with choruses. I said that we all know Beethoven holds an A in the *Ninth Symphony*. But the music is just screaming for it. If you want choruses to sound good while performing music, you're already in dangerous territory when you hit a G. It was fascinating to me, the way this man learned from everything that he heard and everything that he did. He studied in Vienna, then in Israel with European teachers (he was brought to Israel as the Nazis were conquering Europe), and then he served in the British Army, touring as an accompanist in classical music. After World War II he went to Juilliard and within two years became a member of the faculty because his talent was so outstanding.

One thing that was reinforced by him to me was what it means to be a professional in music—also what it means to be a professional composer. Darius Milhaud said it once, when asked why he seems to write so much—"Because that's what a composer does. He doesn't just sit around and wait for inspiration to come. You are a composer, so you write." Many people criticized him for that, saying he wrote too many unimportant pieces—but he had a point. That is also how Robert Starer lived his life. I am learning to do that even now in my own life.

The important thing is, if you want to be a composer, you should set the time to write. This I also learned from William Schuman, who at 27 told the board at Juilliard he would not take the job unless he could come in at 11:00, so that he could write music in the morning.

— 23 —

GERSHON KINGSLEY

Gershon Kingsley is one of the most gifted musicians that I've ever had the pleasure of encountering and befriending in my lifetime. I'm not sure how we met the first time, but I became aware of his music and performed several of his works over the years. Many of them had pop music or jazz influences, even though his training, as far as I know, was all classical. He has been a pianist, and has also conducted several musicals on Broadway.

He still gets commissioned today to do industrial commercials. One of his greatest claims to fame was that when the Moog synthesizer came into being, he started experimenting with it, and was one of the first ones to do anything with it commercially. As a result, the famed Saul Hurok came to him and said, "I want to present you in a few weeks in a quartet of Moog synthesizers in Carnegie Hall." As Kingsley put it, "There wasn't anyone else I knew who could *play* the Moog synthesizer." So he took three pianists that he knew, trained them to play the instrument, and they performed the concerts.

He wrote many choral works. One of them is *What is Man?* I had the pleasure of doing the premiere of it at Avery Fischer Hall, and the Narrator was Hal Holbrook. Our paths crossed here and there over the years, and then something very funny happened.

A few years ago while I was living in Seattle, Kinglsey said to me that he was going to Germany, but had to conduct a twentieth anniversary concert of his *Rock* service at a synagogue in Jersey. He was the first to write a rock service for a synagogue. It is very beautiful, by the way. He asked me if I was interested in guest conducting it, as he was unable to return from Germany in time to conduct it, and so I did that too.

As I mentioned before, his claim to fame is a tune that he wrote on the Moog synthesizer, a famous piece called *Popcorn*. It has a very unique sound—everyone knows this one. Nowadays you hear it played on cell phones, and he is still collecting royalties. He told me that a hundred and fifty different arrangements and orchestrations have been made of it around the world.

I so much admire Kingsley's enthusiasm for music. The man is in his eighties now, and he is still writing as if his life depended on it. Right now he is busy writing a big opera. I love his zest for life, his zest for music. Occasionally I have arguments with him when he downplays his own work *Popcorn*, saying that he wants to write more "serious" music.

There's a story that Brahms was walking along the Danube, and saw a couple of lovers walking along. The boy was whistling a theme from Schubert. He said, "This is my dream, that I'll be walking along and that someone will just be whistling a theme from one of my compositions." There are people whistling Kingsley tunes every day without his even knowing it. He is one of the most versatile musicians on the planet, and in this regard is similar to giants like Leonard Bernstein.

− 24 −

JAN PIERCE

Jan Pierce was a cantor with a very beautiful voice, who also played the violin and sang in a band. One day, he got an engagement in Radio City Music Hall, and somebody heard him singing. The person told Toscanini that he *must* go and see this man. After hearing the performance, every time Toscanini had an opera part that he thought suitable, he called up Pierce. So Toscanini essentially discovered Pierce, who became one of the more famous opera tenors at the Metropolitan Opera.

I got a call one day from Pierce, saying, "I am making a recording of Rosh Hashanah music. I have already commissioned arrangements for it, and am wondering if you would be interested in doing the recording." I was delighted and accepted. A wonderful friendship developed after the recording.

I was amazed at what good shape his voice was in (he was seventy or so at the time). He explained that he'd quit for a year or so when he thought his voice was going sour, and ended up going to his eighty-year-old opera coach, who helped him get back into shape. I asked how he managed to stay in such fantastic shape—especially as a tenor, in his seventies. He said to me, "I don't use my capital—I just use the dividends."

In the second session of the recording, a short bubbly, very beautiful woman approached us, who happened to be his wife, Alice. Jan Pierce had apparently told his wife about me. "I want you to meet my wife," he said to me, to which she jumped in and said, "I had to come and see for myself the conductor that he didn't fight with." He apparently had told everyone that I was one person he had never had a fight with!

We actually did have a misunderstanding in the first session. In one of the pieces, a place in the music indicated *fermata* (hold). We came to that point, and I held the *fermata*—he was holding a very high note. This went for a while, and it got to the point where he couldn't hold any longer. So he stopped and shouted, "Why don't you move on?!" I said, "I am waiting for you—you are the soloist!" He replied, "I'm waiting for *you*." That was the extent of our squabble, if you can even call it that.

We immediately hit it off musically. Of course, the only other conductor that we knew in the past that Pierce never fought with was Arturo Toscanini, who discovered him, and with whom he made many recordings, such as the Verdi *Requiem*.

Years later, when we met again a few times, I heard the story that Kingsley used to tour with Jan Pierce as his accompanist. According to Kingsley, and I can believe it, Jan Pierce was a little bit tight with money, and didn't really pay that well. The reason that I got the call to do the recording at the last minute was because Kingsley was originally going to do the recording but quit the job at the last minute because he was so angry with Pierce.

Jan Pierce used to tell anecdotes better than anyone I know. He was an observant Jew, and very often near the holidays he'd get calls from all sorts of organizations around Miami, where retired people were living who didn't have any family. There would be a Seder with three- to four-hundred people. Because he was Jewish, they often asked him to volunteer his services to the synagogues during the Seder. Telling the story, Pierce recounted, "Finally one day, I said to the man on the phone—do you know how I make a living to support my family?" The man on the other end was silent. He said, "I sing. If I sing to support my family, I *can't* volunteer my services."

He lived in New Rochelle, New York. He said, "One day I was working in the garden and decided that instead of praying at home, I would walk to the temple, which wasn't far away. I had been working in the garden, and when I arrived the sexton stopped me at the door and told me that I couldn't enter the temple with the clothes that I was wearing. I said, "What are you talking about?" He said, "Tell me Mr. Pierce, if you went to a business meeting with a very important person, wouldn't you dress up?" Pierce walked back home, took a shower, got dressed, and headed back. That was Pierce—he would learn from any situation and anybody.

One day I got a call from Jan. "Abe—Jan Pierce. Did you see me already in *Fiddler on the Roof*?" I said "No," but I was afraid to tell him that I hadn't even heard he'd gotten the role. "I haven't had a chance yet." He said, "When are you coming?" I gave him a date, and he said that he'd have tickets waiting for me, and that he expected me to come backstage to see him after the performance. He said "And this time, I'll be able to see your ugly face!" He had just had a cornea operation and could see! So we went to see him in *Fiddler on the Roof.* I'd seen the show with so many others, but Pierce added some things that nobody could have done as well, since he had such a personal understanding of the life and role.

− 25 −

WILLIAM STEINBERG

I am reminded of a wonderful saying that I heard from William Steinberg, who I adore. I prepared for him several times the choruses for the New York Philharmonic when he was guest conducting. One piece was Beethoven's *Missa Solemnis*. It was also with the Collegiate Chorale. He came to the first piano rehearsal, and afterwards emerged elated at what he had heard. He said to me, "This was terrific! I'm glad that nobody told them that it was difficult." It sounds funny, but there is truth to it. If a conductor keeps telling the chorus that a piece is difficult, instead of teaching them to do the things that would inherently counter the difficulty, he ends up fulfilling his own prophecy.

I met William Steinberg at the Aspen Summer School of Music in 1954. When I finished the conservatory in Israel and prepared the Radio and Conservatory Chorus for Darius Milhaud's *David*, I received a recommendation that earned me a scholarship from the America-Israel Foundation to go to Aspen before starting at Juilliard in September.

That year, Steinberg happened to be the teacher for orchestral conducting in Aspen. Afterwards, we lost touch for a while, but in 1961, when I was preparing choruses for the New York Philharmonic, he guest-conducted several times and we reconnected.

In the first instance, I prepared the Britten *War Requiem*, and the

Missa Solemnis. For some reason we struck up a great friendship. From him I heard so many wonderful stories about Toscanini, whom he referred to as "the old man," including a story that had to do with the pronunciation of Latin.

In the U.S.A., we use the version of pronunciation of Latin that is known as Church Latin. For all practical purposes, this is an Italian version of Latin. The story that I heard from Steinberg was as follows:

"You know I was an assistant to Toscanini when I was twenty-one years old. He was rehearsing the Verdi *Requiem*, and I said to him at one point, 'Maestro, I studied Latin at a University in Germany, and the pronunciation that they are using here is absolutely wrong.' He turned to me and said, 'Tell me young man, do you think that the ancient Romans pronounced Latin the way the Germans do it today or the way the Italians do?'" Steinberg said, "I thought about it, and never asked any questions again about Latin pronunciation."

In a word, he was a sensational musician. As a matter of fact in many ways, his recordings of Beethoven's symphonies are my favorites. I think he did all nine on Vanguard records, and they are superb. As a conductor, he is so true to the score, because he is an adorer of music. You hear his heart in it—he loved music. Very unsentimental, but full of sentiment.

Once, when Steinberg was conducting an overture by Robert Starer, he opened with a large cymbal crash in the score. He kept reproaching himself, saying "What kind of an amateur are you?" I asked what had happened, and he said, "I was giving the opening beat and I dislocated my shoulder! If I had done it as an eighteen-year-old, that would be one thing. But I should know better by now!"

– 26 –

CHARLES MUNCH

Charles Munch was the music director of the Boston Symphony for many, many years while I was still a student at Juilliard. I also saw him when I went to Tanglewood to study Orchestral Conducting, taught by Eleazar deCavallo. As the director of the Boston Symphony I thought he was fantastic, especially when conducting French music. He was very French—very *charming* French. He was really a wonderful conductor, especially in pieces like Maurice Ravel's *Daphnis et Chloe*.

I had a chance to prepare *Daphnis et Chloe* later for him when he conducted the New York Philharmonic. Years later I prepared the same work for Pierre Boulez, and it was such a study in contrast. Munch was so tired at that time in his life. He cut one of the last rehearsals at the time saying, "You know it, I know it—we don't need to continue." The truth of the matter was that the Boston Symphony knew the piece well because they did it quite often under him. The New York Philharmonic, on the other hand, hadn't done it in at least twenty years, and they were grumbling about the fact that they needed another rehearsal.

As a conductor, Boulez was very exacting. He stopped on every other chord, tuning the orchestra and so forth. One could say in the Munch version there was even a little bit of confusion toward the end, because it was a difficult piece to keep together metrically. But when I now compare the performances between these two men, there is not even a comparison. Charles Munch, to my ear, conducted the piece as Ravel heard it.

The principal thing that I learned from working with Munch is that the character of the music is much more important than the details. When one gets on the podium to perform a piece, it is the character that one should have in mind—not individual notes.

– 27 –

KURT ADLER

Kurt Adler was the Director General of the San Francisco Opera. I went to California twice for six weeks with my family during the summers of 1974 and 1975 to guest-conduct in their summer program, which included choral music. The first time came about in the most interesting way. I received a call in New York City from a man whose last name was very famous in the conducting world, Rodzinski. (His uncle or father was Arthur Rodzinski, the music director of the New York Philharmonic.) He said, "I'm the assistant to Mr. Kurt Adler, the Director of the San Francisco Opera. During the summer we have a special program called the Merola program, and Mr. Adler had an idea of doing the *St. Matthew Passion* on stage, theatrically. He wanted to know what you think about that." My immediate reaction was that this was the best idea I'd heard in many, many years. He was apparently very surprised, because everyone else he'd asked had told him it was the wrong thing to do. Since I was director of Choral Music at Juilliard and had a good reputation, he was delighted to find out that I endorsed the idea. He asked if I would come and guest conduct the performance. I told him I would be delighted.

He asked me to do the favor of convincing the Stage Director from the City Opera of New York. He was not yet convinced, but Kurt Adler believed that if I could help to convince him, he would be the perfect person to stage it. I agreed to persuade him with my understanding of the dramatic content and emphases that fill the piece from the first to the last note.

And so it was—I called the gentleman, whose name I can't remember, and he came to our apartment. We had a three hour discussion about the proposition. The nice thing about him was that he was already a singer and a good musician—and so we were able to really delve into the music. After the three hours, I suggested only two specific things with respect to the staging. The one that I remember is as follows: One of the climaxes in the passion is when the crowds are calling for the crucifixion of Jesus, and they suddenly realize that He is the Son of God. They sing two short measures of music to "Truly this was the Son of God, the Son of God." These two measures are probably the most beautiful measures in the entire piece. I said that if I had my choice on how to stage it, that the audience would be in the dark up to that point, and then, when the chorus started in, that the lights subtly, in an unperceivable way, would begin to illuminate. By the end of the measures the entire auditorium would be illuminated. The gentleman agreed, and the end result was fantastic.

The two of us went to San Francisco and rehearsed for six weeks. This was one of the highlights of my musical career. Apparently Adler was very happy with the results. After the performance, he came backstage and paid me a wonderful compliment. While complimenting me he gave a little jab at German conductor, Herbert Von Karajan. He said to me, "You know this summer I went to Vienna, and saw 'god' himself (Karajan) conducting the *St. Matthew Passion*. He used three organs and two orchestras. With all of this, your performance was much, much better."

Then, Adler made something of a mistake—years ago he commissioned Carlisle Floyd to write a piece of music to Steinbeck's

Of Mice and Men. When he received the music of the commissioned work, he apparently didn't like it, and didn't perform it. A few years later, the Seattle Opera decided to do the premiere. It was quite a success, and has been performed several times since.

A few years after my first encounter, I received another call in New York, and was asked if I'd like to come the following summer to perform a Handel opera. I must admit that I already had a prejudice, because of the ones I'd already looked at I had found them all very, very boring. And I realized that the reason he suggested to me to do one of Handel's operas was that after the *St. Matthew's Passion*, I was becoming typecast as a Baroque specialist. I told him that I would rather not do it, and so Rodzinski offered me the alternative of conducting *Of Mice and Men.* I was unaware of Adler's history with this piece, but knew the composer and said, "Absolutely." I came the next summer and found out that he had not hired enough strings to balance the rest of the orchestra. Then I heard the background story of how he missed out by not doing the world premiere, and I decided that whether subconsciously or consciously, Adler was probably hoping that the piece would fail, to prove his initial feelings true. He started doing things that he never did the first time I worked with him, although people had warned me—he started interrupting my rehearsals, saying that the balance was not good. I turned to him and told him that if he would hire some more strings, it would balance better. Anyhow, we did our best, and in spite of the challenges with Adler, the opera was a great success in San Francisco too.

In terms of the *St. Matthew Passion,* Adler took a creative risk in staging the production. Tthere was a big headline and entire page in the San Francisco Examiner in advance of the concert, reading, "How can a conductor of Abraham Kaplan's caliber lend his name to such a blasphemy?" The article continued, explaining why we could not possibly do a good job. There was a huge controversy. But Adler had such a huge following in San Francisco, that no matter what he decided to do, no matter how out of the ordinary, people would come to watch the performance.

I came to have great respect for the above-mentioned critic, because after the concert when the review came out, he actually admitted that he had been wrong.

Adler was a wonderful musician with very discriminating tastes. He had his own convictions, and was not afraid to live by these. That is why when he didn't like *Of Mice and Men* (he knew immediately just from the score) and was willing to let someone else do the premiere.

− 28 −

MARTINA ARROYO

I scheduled a performance of Rossini's *Stabat Mater* at Avery Fischer Hall, and asked Martina Arroyo's manager if she would like to sing the soprano solo. Her manager told me that she was planning to go to Europe, but that she could probably stay in town another two weeks to perform with me.

As a result, while she was staying in New York, awaiting that performance, a soprano became sick at the Metropolitan Opera—they asked Arroyo, who had performed the piece before, to perform as an emergency substitute. In many ways, that little incident jump-started her career in the United States. Many American singers have gone to Europe in order to gain popularity before trying to get into the Met, but Arroyo happened to be in the right place at the right time.

She was so sweet, humble and complimentary to the other musicians. While she was sitting at the rehearsal of the *Stabat Mater*, resting her voice, I asked one of the soloists from the chorus to sing the solo in her place. When the rehearsal was over, Arroyo said to me, "What a fantastic singer—I'm glad I got the job!"

She was a wonderful singer who was very, very musical. For many at that time, due to lingering stereotypes, it was remarkable to see an African-American sing the Italian repertoire as passionately as she did.

− 29 −

HANS REHFUSS

Hans Rehfuss gave me my first taste, as a young conductor in Israel, of working with a top-caliber professional singer.

In order to commemorate the three thousand year history of Jerusalem, the Israeli government had commissioned Darius Milhaud to write an opera. Milhaud wrote a composition entitled, *David*.

Half of the composition, which was about three and a half hours long, was a solo by the main character, David, in Hebrew. I couldn't believe what I was hearing. After preparing the chorus, I sat dumbfounded, listening to this man from Switzerland who had just received the score in the mail. He sang in Hebrew with perfect diction, and did not make a single mistake on a single note.

I thought, "This must be what it is like to work with a professional singer!" However, I discovered soon thereafter that there weren't too many singers like Hans Rehfuss—he was one of the best that I have ever had the privilege of working with, and I later realized that he had done a lot of recordings with different symphonies and philharmonic orchestras around the world. Although I have had opportunities since then to work with many of the world's most talented singers, I never forgot Rehfuss.

A few years later, Rehfuss surprised and humbled me with a phone call. He came to this country, and of course had aged. I believe he had retired by choice, because his voice was still in terrific shape. He had moved to the United States and had a University job. He called me and asked if I remembered him, to which I replied "Of course."

He asked me to write a recommendation letter for him…I was fairly unfamiliar with the procedures at the time, and I was very upset that a University would not have the brains to realize that they had an international star under their noses. Anyhow, I wrote him the highest of recommendations. I have no idea if he got the job, but while I had him on the phone, I asked if he would perform the Brahms Requiem with me at Carnegie Hall, which he obliged.

As a musician, Rehfuss could prepare even a new, contemporary work and know it like the back of his hand by the first rehearsal… but most impressive was that he had one of the most attractive and mellifluous baritone voices that I've ever heard.

— 30 —

CARLO MARIA GIULINI

When performing with the New York Philharmonic, Carlo Maria Giulini chose the *Quattro Petzzi Sacrae*. Since *Te Deum* starts a capella, the first movement is a cappella, and is very difficult to keep in tune, he said right in the beginning that he wanted the chorus to start half a step higher, so that by the time they got to the end, they would come exactly to the right pitch. And it worked! This was his choice, and again, the sum of his experience. I found it fascinating.

I heard an interview with him on the radio later, while he was music director for the Los Angeles Philharmonic. The interviewer asked him, "How do you approach the study of a new musical score? Do you first analyze the form, do you first sing through the main tunes, or do you play it?" So he said, like a typically wonderful Italian, "It's not always the same way … it is like falling in love. You go somewhere and see a beautiful woman across the way. So you try to get to know her. In other cases, you take your time and watch from afar, etc…" Anyhow, he was delightful, and his response was very revealing of his personality.

It was actually a big surprise when he became the Los Angeles Philharmonic conductor, though he only stayed for a short time. It was a surprise because he was very well known, and most people knew that he wasn't interested in becoming a music director of any symphony orchestra. He was happy with guest conducting, perhaps because he didn't like the administrative part of a directorship, which can be quite burdensome. He was good enough to sustain a fantastic career with only guest conducting.

Also, music directorship in the United States is not only administrative, but it also requires a fundraising role. He would have to go to certain fundraising events, and European conductors especially were not used to that. He is the only one that I ever knew who made it a matter of principal that he didn't want to be a musical director.

– 31 –

ZUBIN MEHTA

While I was collaborating with the New York Philharmonic, Zubin Mehta was invited to come and conduct a memorial service at St. Patrick's Cathedral. He chose to do the Verdi *Te Deum* from the *Quattro Petzzi Sacrae*. I was director of choral music at Juilliard and prepared choirs for the New York Philharmonic at the time, so he asked if I would bring the Camerata Singers to perform with him. This was long before he became music director of the New York Philharmonic—by the time he did that, I had already moved to Seattle, Washington.

He was very pleasant to work with, but I was amazed by how businesslike he was with conducting. I don't know why, I guess I expected something different.

There was something very interesting that he adopted. The *Te Deum* usually has a little problem after about five or ten minutes of music, because it starts a capella, and eventually the orchestra comes in. Having everyone remain in key is always a difficulty—he didn't even want to wait to find out if they would still be in tune—he had his own solution. He doubled the bass part with double basses from the orchestra, which I thought was an ingenious idea. You almost couldn't hear them, and they produced overtones that kept the chorus exactly in tune.

– 32 –

JOSEPH SZIGETI

I once went to a recital that Szigeti gave in a very small auditorium at a museum. It probably seated ninety people at the most, on folding chairs. He was already an old man at the time, but was a legendary violinist, and I thought it would be a crime to miss the opportunity.

He started to play, and I noticed that he played a lot of glissandos and *portomentos* (sliding up and down in pitch). I knew that it was the style of the first part of the twentieth century and definitely the end of the nineteenth century, but I must say that since my ear was not used to it, it was extremely painful to sit through. Nevertheless, I insisted on remaining in my seat—besides, it would have been embarrassing to leave that small auditorium. An amazing thing happened to me in the process. In about five to ten minutes I got used to the style, and realized what a phenomenal musician he was, which confirmed an opinion that I had in the abstract before—that some of those things like glissandos, which some critics called "schmaltz," are really just a matter of fashion. Every generation seems to switch to another fashion. One has to go beyond those peripheral things and concentrate on the actual music-making. When one is listening to a performer, one should try to get over the external mannerisms…and just listen to the music-making. One gets rewarded—in this case I heard one of the greatest musicians of his time, making real music.

I had an experience related to this years later, when I was auditioning soloists at Juilliard for the Verdi *Requiem*. I had a wonderful soprano soloist, and we came to the point where Verdi writes, *portamento*. The soloist was to start at the very high note and slide down to the low note. Of course it was not fashionable at the time, but the soloist hit the high note very purely, and then cleanly sang down to the low note, sounding more like she was singing Mozart. She was a wonderful musician, in addition to being a beautiful singer. I said, "But Veronica—Verdi said *portamento*." She blushed, asking, "Do you really want that?" I replied, "Whether I want it or not is really not important—*Verdi* wrote, *portamento!*"

It demonstrated to me that here were two wonderful musicians who were part of their time and culture—fifty years apart—and they each had their own wonderful style and preferences.

It is not unlike when you see a period piece or historical play—people are wearing "funny clothes," but this is not the main point of the story, it is just a stylistic element. You have to see through to the humanity of the story in order to truly appreciate and enjoy the performance.

— 33 —

RANDALL THOMPSON

Randall Thompson is probably the premier American choral music composer. When I was teaching at the New York State Summer School of the Arts in Chautauqua, New York, I devoted the concert one summer to the music of Randall Thompson. He was already a very old man, he could barely see, and yet, he was extremely gracious. In many ways he was the favorite choral composer of Sergei Koussevitski.

I invited him as my guest—to come to the concert, and to conduct any part of the concert that he wanted to. He ended up conducting only one piece, which surprised me. I was absolutely sure he'd want to conduct more pieces with chorus and orchestra. He must have been in his eighties at the time, and came with an assistant who helped him walk.

To illustrate his humility - when I told him that the *Alleluia* that he wrote for the opening exercises of the Berkshire Music Center was one of the greatest pieces ever written for a cappella choral music, he said, "Oh no, your *Alleluia* is much better." It was not true, but it was very gracious of him to say.

– 34 –

LUKAS FOSS

Foss was a composer who was greatly admired by musicians like Stravinsky and Bernstein. I conducted his piece, entitled *Fragments of Archilocus,* at Philharmonic Hall, and the man drove me absolutely crazy. As with any composer in a rehearsal, I turned to him after each run-through to see if he had suggestions. Most composers sit back and hold off on their commentary until in private with the conductor, unless they have a quick suggestion that might be helpful in the rehearsal. Foss actually walked up to the podium, and began to rehearse the choir and change things. The chorus was a good chorus, but not professional—so he was having a difficult time changing things as quickly as he wanted to. I actually don't remember the performance, but I would be willing to bet that it was less than wonderful, and that the chorus would have been better off if our rehearsal had been left alone. The experience shattered my theory that "good composers" who were sure of themselves did not fuss around with the performers. In this case, Foss was a marvelous composer—but it was just not in his temperament to leave things alone.

— 35 —

MADELINE MARSHALL

Madeline Marshall was the English Diction teacher at the Juilliard School. Underneath this modest title was a superb musician and concert pianist. She'd had a solo career prior to teaching, and in fact I had heard that she had performed a piano concerto with Arturo Toscanini. At some point, in spite of what would have been a brilliant solo career, she opted to settle down, get married, and have children. So she took the professorship at Juilliard, and continued as an accompanist, mainly coaching singers throughout the years.

Madeline had a wonderful ear for languages. When I arrived in New York as a student of Choral Conducting, I was delighted to find out that all of the singers and choral conductors were required to take diction and language classes in four languages: German, Italian, French, and English. When I went to her class I realized that my dreams were fulfilled, because I'd previously conducted amateur choirs for five years, and a professional chorus for Israeli radio for a year. I didn't realize it, but I was starved to do something constructive with the language of choral pieces, in addition to the music itself.

From the very first class I realized that in addition to improving my English, I found many, many answers to things that I had struggled with during my work with the Radio Chorus. I had been conducting and recording every two weeks, and the next frontier was manipulating diction to enhance the sound, to make the meaning clearer in an effortless way. Here I found the class and the teacher who not only knew how to do it, but who systematized it for the English language. Her most skeptical students were of course many of the American voice majors, who thought it was silly for someone to teach them their own language. Prepared for that reaction from students, Madeline would pull a marvelous stunt at the beginning of each year. She would ask members of the class to say their names, or to articulate a typical sentence that they might use during the day. By their accent, she could tell within a radius of fifty miles where they came from. She did this mainly for the Americans, and it impressed them—the bright ones realized quickly the great benefit of such a skill. The less bright ones just thought it was an interesting stunt, but failed to realize its relevance for them as musicians. The knowledge of how to treat the different elements of the language in singing is the key to making the text clear to the audience, and also to beautifying the sound. The sound that the voice produces is a mixture of the pitch and the syllable of text being sung. Knowing how to affect not only the music, but also the text gives the musician an additional tool to make the sound of the chorus more beautiful, and also to make it possible for the audience to understand the text in an effortless way. Although I passed her course very well the first time, I learned so much that I asked permission to take it again the following year.

Her method of teaching English diction, in addition to following assignments from her book, was to ask each one of us to prepare a song, an aria, folk song…any song. She would sit at the piano, accompany our song, and then interrupt with helpful suggestions. In addition to general English Diction (lyric diction, as it was sometimes called,) she gave personal coaching in the class. When it was my turn, I decided to bring in a long folk song with twelve verses, since I was getting so much out of this class. I assumed that she would stop me partway, because it was so long, but I would sing for as long as she needed in order to coach me. The problem with this song was that it had a refrain with a problematic "ee" sound for a non-native speaker. I decided that I would concentrate on that vowel, and hoped to pronounce it well. I began singing, and felt like I was going on forever without an interruption. By the sixth verse, I found myself wondering why she wasn't saying anything, and I looked across the room at my fellow students. They appeared very tense— especially during the part of the refrain that had the sentence, "with the sheets turned down." Apparently, I was mistakenly pronouncing the "ee" sound like the "i" vowel in the word, "city"! When six or seven verses went by and she did not stop me, I looked out of the corner of my eye at Madeline Marshall, red as a beet, with tears rolling down her eyes, and trying as hard as she could not to laugh. I finally stopped and asked everyone… "Why don't you laugh already?" …to which the room burst into hysterical laughter. Madeline hadn't been able to bring herself to tell me, for fear of this laughter, but it was one of the funniest moments of my student years at Juilliard.

We remained friends for a long time. When I returned to the United States, before Juilliard had a chance to hire me, she asked me to teach a master class. Madeline taught at the Union Theological Seminary and the seminary hired me to be a professor of choral music (1961-1974), until years later when they closed their music department and moved it to Yale. Before they closed the department, it was the largest graduate music school in the Protestant church, and for a few years, three members of the faculty including myself used to tour to different cities and give master classes in our respective disciplines.

Madeline and I formed something of a mutual admiration society. I cherished her friendship, and probably learned from her more about music than I did from any teacher in my lifetime. As a result, in my conducting book, she is the only person that I mention by name.

– 36 –

CLAUDIO ABBADO

My first memory of Claudio Abbado was when the three winners of the Mitropolous Conducting Competition shared a concert conducting the New York Philharmonic. During the final rehearsal I was standing in the auditorium next to Bernstein. At one point, when Abbado was conducting, Bernstein whispered to me, "I wish I had that kind of legato." As was typical of Bernstein, he immediately identified the greatest strength of Abbado's conducting, and was generous enough to acknowledge it.

I had two subsequent opportunities to collaborate with Abbado: Once, preparing Beethoven's *Symphony No. 9*, and the other, Stravinsky's *Oedopus Rex*. His conducting of the latter, completely from memory, left me in great awe of his talents, because it was assured, spectacular, and devoid of unhealthy tension.

– 37 –

BEVERLY SILLS

I never had the pleasure of actually working with Beverly Sills, but I did have the pleasure of making her acquaintance in a unique circumstance. I was commissioned by the Crystal Cathedral ministry, headed by Dr. Robert Schuller, to write a composition for the opening of the Cathedral. One day I received an invitation to come to a pre-opening recital by Beverly Sills at the Cathedral, which was still under construction. What was even more frightening for me as a musician was the fact that the sound system was not finished. Poor Beverly Sills had to sing a concert with all of the windows rattling, accompanied only by a piano—it must have been exhausting! The whole experience gave me insight into Schuller's amazing organization and ability to raise funds, because every panel in that Cathedral was sponsored by somebody. Contributions qualified donors to have their names engraved on seats or wall panels, and there were thousands of panels. Anyhow, I digress. Before the recital, we were riding the elevator with Dr. Schuller and Beverly Sills - I recognized her immediately but I had no idea if she knew who I was, since we had never been formally introduced and I had never spoken to her.

Of course I knew who she was, as I had seen her pictures in the paper many times. She *might* have seen my pictures in the papers because I was very active at the time, but clearly we had never met.

To my astonishment, she turned to me in the elevator and said, "Abe, what are you doing here?! So good to see you!" We hugged, and when we hugged she whispered to me, not so softly, "What's a nice Jewish boy like you doing in a place like this?!" So I said, "Well, I've been commissioned to write some choral pieces for the opening of the Cathedral. And I might ask you the same question!" And she said, "My mother listens to Dr. Schuller every Sunday, and she adores his positive message. She is a big contributor, so they knew they could ask me to do a fundraising event for them, as it would make my mother so very happy!"

That was a short, delightful experience with Beverly Sills, who was very much in person, like her industry nickname, Bubbles. When we met, she was bubbling with happiness. What I found even more amazing was that bubbly nature in spite of several tragedies she had had in her life. She raised a daughter who could not hear from birth. Her own daughter, so close to her, was never able to hear her mother's music—the thing that Beverly Sills excelled at and that was so important to her in life. For some reason she was capable, in spite of all the difficulties that she faced, to be an amazing woman, not only as an artist but as a human being.

− 38 −

KARL HAAS

My meeting with Karl Haas was, I thought at the time, purely accidental. But upon second look, forty or fifty years later, I'm having second thoughts. Perhaps it was planned or initiated by him. I was invited to a small dinner party at the house of Joanna Simon and her husband. She was a classical singer and the sister of songwriter and singer, Carly Simon. At this dinner party, I met Karl Haas and his wife. I went to very few parties because I hate small talk, but this was a very intimate party, and Joanna Simon had appeared with me as an alto soloist in many concerts, and in fact, in one that was particularly dear to me. There were only about ten people at the dinner, and Karl turned to me and said, "You know I do a radio program called Adventures in Good Music. I never have guests on it, but I want to do a program which will be about choral music, and I would like you to be a guest host with me, and share the program because of your background." It sounded like a good fit to me because I was very active in New York, as conductor of symphonic/choral music, a capella music, and preparations for the New York Philharmonic.

Haas was a spectacular musician himself, (he was a student of the legendary pianist, Artur Schnabel) and he was always at the edge of discovering emerging and great artists. For example, with great conviction, he mentioned Yo-Yo Ma to me before his name ever appeared in the papers. In later years I learned to trust his amazing instinct. When we finished our program, discussing choral music and what goes into making beautiful choral music, Haas had a surprise for me. We recorded the program at the studios of WQXR in New York, which was the New York Times radio station. I had thought it was only broadcast in New York, but it turned out that it was a syndicated program originating in Cleveland where he was originally from, and was broadcast all over the country.

At the end of the interview he said, "I've just learned you've been moonlighting as a composer. We have the recording you've just made, so why don't you choose a selection to play for our audience, and then we can talk about it." Thinking that I was live, not recorded, I quickly scrambled in my head to chose one or two numbers from my recording, *Glorious*, that I had just finished in England. We played the pieces and discussed them on the air. The biggest surprise was that in subsequent years, until his recent passing, he continued to play selections from Glorious, and from other compositions of mine which I recorded. That first meeting developed into a wonderful friendship. In addition to being an amazing musician, he was a wonderful storyteller, a raconteur. As a matter of fact, I credit him with telling me a joke that passed muster with my family at home. It was the first and only time that my children, who usually said, "Oh Dad, stop telling jokes, you are bad at it!" actually laughed and said something like, "That's a good one!" He told the following story about Artur Schnabel:

> Schnabel, like the artists of his time, used to give an annual recital in Carnegie Hall. And in what became almost a ritual, every time he walked on stage, there was in the first row an attractive gray-haired lady who would applaud enthusiastically before he started, and then a few minutes into the recital, she would fall sound asleep. When he finished a selection, the applause would wake her up. This

went on year after year. Finally one year, while taking a bow, Schnabel bowed a little deeper and said, "Lady, I'm sorry, I tried to play as softly as I could."

The second story he told me was about the friendship between Schnabel and Albert Einstein:

> Einstein was often invited to dine at the Schnabel's house, and he brought his violin and begged Schnabel to read with him through violin and piano sonatas. Schnabel loved the man, so he suffered through it. At one such dinner they began to read through some sonatas. Apparently Einstein made some mistakes, and Schnabel could finally take it no more, slammed down the piano lid, and said, "Albert, can't you count?"

When *Amadeus* came out, first as a play in New York City, I asked Karl if he had seen it. There had been reviews that pointed out its historical inaccuracies. He said, "I don't want to see it." I asked, "Why, because it's historically incorrect?" He replied, "No, because of one thing which *is* historically correct. I know, and I've always known, that Mozart had a very strange laugh. To me, there is beauty that comes out of every bar of Mozart. So I don't want to hear the strange laugh!" And that's when I realized the difference between Haas and myself, and also between myself and many musicians—I was always fascinated by the human foibles of some of these great people. I found it an even greater miracle that such heavenly, perfect music came out of them, and yet, they were regular human beings. If they had been angels or superhuman, there wouldn't have been anything miraculous about it.

This was part of the wonderful legacy Karl Haas left with me, from a generation of musicians that I didn't have the pleasure of meeting personally, and I'm grateful to him for that.

– 39 –

GEORG SOLTI

When it comes to philosophies of how to approach conducting, I was torn from childhood on, between the two extremes of Arturo Toscanini and one of the older generation of conductors (whose name I can't remember.) Toscanini was asked how come he almost always conducted from memory. His serious answer was because his eyesight had gotten bad, but his flippant answer, which many thought was part of his philosophy of conducting and was expressed in his strong performances, was that it's better to have the score in your head rather than your head in the score while conducting.

I think it was Otto Klemperer who was asked why he always conducted from the score, in spite of his wonderful musical memory. His flippant answer was, "I know how to read a score!" He meant that just because someone stood there without a score in front of him, and essentially said to the public, "Look Ma, no hands," it did not mean that they knew the music well.

I personally was leaning towards the Toscanini approach of conducting from memory, and it may have been a mistake on my part. I realized what a terrible mistake it could have been when I met Sir Georg Solti. I think I prepared Beethoven's *Symphony No. 9* for him, which I had prepared for George Szell, Bernstein, and numerous others, including myself. Still, I couldn't memorize the Symphony. I've conducted his *Symphony No. 1* from memory, but the *Ninth Symphony* was too much for me, and so I always had to conduct from the score. When I saw Solti conduct it, even though he appeared physically awkward, almost as if he didn't have a physical aptitude for it, he also had his head constantly buried in the score. I found him to be one of the few conductors whose performances were continuously musical. There were no boring, dead, meaningless stretches of music. While I've seen conductors with great musical memory who have conducted from memory quite easily, they conducted concerts that would put you to sleep, even with the great masterpieces. Solti, on the other hand, was an example of how one could conduct with his head buried in the score and still make music with the best of them. Toward the end of his life Solti said that he was studying Bach's *St. John Passion* and that he was having a great deal of fun. He attributed the enjoyment to the fact that he was a slow learner, and was able to work on it for quite a long time. Through his example, Solti contributed quite a bit to the enrichment of my inner life as a conductor.

– 40 –

ERICH LEINSDORF

I had encounters with Erich Leinsdorf several times. The first time was when I decided to go to Tanglewood as a student and major in orchestral conducting. Originally, I had gone there to study choral conducting, but this was several years later, and it was the year when Leinsdorf was appointed director of the Boston Symphony. With the job came the directorship of Boston Symphony summer home at Tanglewood, which also included a school of music.

I'll never forget his first encounter with the students of orchestral conducting. He threw all kinds of general questions at us. I don't remember if he gave us a written exam or something like it, but he wanted to quiz us to find out the level of students that he had in his class. He began, "I would like you to write down how many trombones are in each of Beethoven's nine symphonies." He wasn't showing off or being superficial—he was just being true to his hard-studying manner. He was a very conscientious musician, and wanted to teach others to be such. Years later I heard that he was contracted by a company to record all of Mozart's forty-one symphonies, and he recorded them all in the studio from memory. He had that kind of temperament and ability. Robert Starer said that Leinsdorf premiered a work of his with the Rochester Symphony, and reported, "I was stunned. I came to the first rehearsal and he was rehearsing the whole piece from memory." A new piece, just written! That's the kind of musician he was.

The next time I encountered him was when he conducted the Bach *B minor Mass* with the New York Philharmonic, and the third time he conducted a Haydn mass. He invited me to his New York apartment to discuss the Haydn mass, which was not one of the more frequently performed masses. He opened a new score, just issued by Bärenreiter, and then proceeded to play the entire score from beginning to end at the piano, stopping only at one spot, and showing me a note in the first violin that was sustained. The chords underneath, however, kept changing. There was no way to explain that note within traditional or classical harmony. He claimed that there was a mistake there, then turned to the title page and read the title, "A Critical Edition." He said, "They should write a non-critical edition, because the least they could do is have a footnote that says, this kind of chord never appears in all of Haydn's music, so something must be wrong here." That was the kind of musician he was; he was amazing in this respect. The testimony of the players who played under him was that he was probably the easiest conductor to play for—no nonsense, he made everything extremely clear, and from stories that I heard, he was one of the two assistants that Toscanini had, the other being Steinberg.

SHLOMO KAPLAN

Left to Right: Abraham Kaplan, Leonard Bernstein, Shlomo Kaplan

I believe that my father, Shlomo Kaplan, was the best choral conductor that I've ever known, bar none—and I don't just say that because he was my father. He intuitively knew what was necessary to make a chorus sound spectacular. Like Bernstein, he was musical "to the bone marrow," as my grandfather used to say.

He must have sung under his father in the synagogue choir when he was a child, very much like I did. As a boy, I sang soprano in his choir. At the age of seventeen (1927), unlike his parents and their generation, he became a Zionist and decided to immigrate to Palestine from Russia to work at whatever profession was available in what was then a desert country. He did all kinds of things that the pioneers did at that time—paved roads, worked in the orange groves. After a short time it became obvious that even in those circumstances they needed somebody to conduct choruses, and after a reasonably short time my father found himself making a living conducting choruses.

After a few years, he brought his entire family to Israel, including his parents, one brother, and two sisters. As a result they survived World War II. As the oldest son, he felt responsible for bringing and supporting his family, and somehow in a small, developing country, he was able to do this through choral conducting, taking on a synagogue chorus, and several community choruses. He made a living good enough to build his family a house, which was quite rare at the time.

He wrote arrangements for chorus, but never wrote original music. Perhaps his greatest sadness was never having had an opportunity to further his studies as a musician in Europe. Whenever there were outstanding musicians who came to Israel, he would always try to study with them for whatever time they were available. As a result of this and a publishing house that he managed as part of the Histadrut (labor union association), he greatly influenced choral music in the early years of the emerging state. Shlomo was the head of its music department, and as such he not only saw to it that Israeli choral compositions were published, but he also had someone translate many of the great works of choral music (Mendelssohn's oratorio *Elijah*, Bach's *Passion*, the *Requiem* by Mozart…) into Hebrew and published them. Through his work and travels, he started what became a choral movement in Israel, where every kibbutz, town and city had its own chorus. The people were nourished by this great music. Instruments were less accessible in a developing country, but choruses could be formed anywhere, and didn't require professional training. As a side note, the Palestine Philharmonic* was formed when most of the musicians from the Berlin Philharmonic were expelled from Germany. They were a world-class orchestra. Many people said that the Berlin Philharmonic was quite poor during World War II, especially in the strings! Although wonderful, the choral work in early Palestine was not performed at quite the same level. When Shlomo had the great choral works translated, he took only a few choruses from those oratorios, masses, etc... Shlomo would often hold seminars for choral conductors from around the whole country, who in turn would teach and perform with choruses in their respective towns. My father adored Toscanini—as did most Jews in Palestine. Since Toscanini was an anti-fascist, spoke against Mussolini, and was considered by many to be the greatest conductor of the day, the Israeli Philharmonic invited him to come and perform its inaugural concert. Somebody was able to sneak my father into those rehearsals, which for him was like a dream come true. Do you know who came to prepare the inaugural concert? Toscanini sent a very young conductor, his protégé, to prepare that orchestra for him—and that conductor was William Steinberg. Later in life, when I heard the many stories about Toscanini from William Steinberg, I almost felt as if we were related.

As a musician, I learned from my father that the most critical thing for a chorus in performance is *breath*. If any musical phrase is not sung with appropriate breath—which starts before you sing, and which lasts at least until the end of the phrase, if not longer—then you can't have good results, no matter how good the vocal training is. Shlomo knew

---

*   It later became the Israeli Philharmonic

this by instinct. Throughout rehearsals he used to say, "You didn't breathe here" or "You need to breathe there." "Stagger the breathing."

I also learned that if a conductor doesn't conduct well, he or she might sabotage the chorus' ability to breathe properly. It is the conductor's responsibility not only to mention the breathing, but also to include it in his own conducting.

As a matter of fact, everything that I ever learned about choral conducting that is worth remembering, I learned from him. The irony of it all is that during my childhood, when I was asked if I would become "a choral conductor like your father?" I always said, "Never."

The first time my father realized that I had been conducting, we were sitting in my living room, listening to the radio. The radio broadcaster announced, "...and now we're going to hear a chorus conducted by Abraham Kaplan." My stepmother, Rachel, turned to Shlomo and said, "Shlomo, they made a mistake! They said Abraham!" Then they both slowly turned to me as if to say, "Wait a minute, is that *you*?"

Later in life, when I was appointed the Director of Choral Music at Juilliard, my father came to visit me. As was the case with Israelis for many years, he was not allowed to bring any substantial dollars out of the country. He lived with me in my New York apartment, and I used to give him an "allowance" so that he would have some spending money. He was so pleased that his son was appointed as the Director of Choral Music at the legendary Juilliard. He would meet some musicians that he knew in New York, and when they asked what he was doing, he would say, "I am visiting my son." When they asked, "What does he do in New York?" My father proudly replied, "He is the Director of Choral Music at Juilliard." With eyes wide open, they would say, "Wait a minute—your son is Abraham Kaplan???" He nonchalantly answered, "Yes, that's my son." When he visited me he said, "There is a God in heaven." If his dream did not come to be during his own life, it came to fruition in his son's life.

When I was preparing the Bach *St. Matthew Passion* for Bernstein, I introduced Shlomo to the choir as my father, and told the chorus that he was going to conduct them. They instinctively knew what I'd told them—that he was the best choral conductor alive.

At some point after World War II in Israel, Shlomo decided to invite Jewish choirs from all over Europe and the U.S. to come to Israel for a festival. All of the Jewish communities that survived the holocaust were interested in visiting this new Jewish state. He commissioned a composer by the name of Chaim Alexander to write a choral composition for the first festival on a text from Isaiah, translated "And I will gather you from all of the nations." Anyhow, sometimes a commission is successful, sometimes not. This time it was wonderful— and it was used as a song for the choruses to learn all around the world. Besides the individual choral concerts, the choruses all came together in Jerusalem and sang that one composition together. Shlomo came to the United States by boat, and returned to Israel together with all of the American choirs. On the boat back to Israel he rehearsed all three- to four-hundred choir members for the commissioned selection. For the next twenty-five years in New York, every time I conducted a concert someone would come to me and say, "You know, I sang for your father on that boat, on the way to the Zimriah* festival."

---

* "Zimriah" is from the Hebrew, "Zemer," which means "to sing."

ADDENDUM:

What Does a Conductor (Maestro) Do…
And Who the Hell Needs Him?

– ADDENDUM: –

WHAT DOES A CONDUCTOR (MAESTRO) DO... AND WHO THE HELL NEEDS HIM?*

A man walks into a parrot shop and sees a sign, "Musical Prodigies For Sale." The prices listed are outrageous. The man asks the proprietor, "Why are you asking $15,000 for this ordinary looking parrot?" The proprietor says quickly, "Judge for yourself!" He takes the parrot out of the cage, hands him a small violin, and the bird plays the Mendelssohn violin concerto like an angel. A second parrot, for $30,000, plays the Dvorak Cello concerto with the warmth reminiscent of Pablo Casals. A third, costing $50,000, plays the piano with the bravado of Artur Rubinstein. The customer is deeply impressed and moves down the line to the final cage, a parrot priced at half a million dollars. "What does this one play and why is the price so high?"

"I don't know, but all the others call him Maestro!"

I recall a Seinfeld episode where Jerry carried on about an orchestral conductor's absolute irrelevance. He waved his arms and flailed about

---

*   For more information pertaining to choral conducting in general, refer to my textbook, *Choral Conducting*, published by W.W. Norton.

in satirical mockery of what seemed to him absolute nonsense. A folk culture icon, Seinfeld undoubtedly touched a nerve with many viewers who similarly have asked themselves, "What does a conductor actually do, anyway?" Herein I will attempt to answer this question, which has perplexed audiences and even musicians for years. What does the conductor actually do for the music? We see the maestro waving his or her arms before a musical ensemble, but it is not always clear what contribution he or she is making to the music. Believe it or not, a Maestro "plays" an instrument called an orchestra, chorus, or band. Why, one might ask, does an orchestra composed of well-trained musicians *need* a Maestro to *play* it? This is simple—because a composition written by *one* composer speaking to *individuals* in the audience needs one *human* pulse to unify its rhythm. The humanity of this pulse is critical—which is why orchestras are not conducted by metronomes or other precise, electronic devices. The way in which the maestro "plays" the ensemble is one of the mysterious miracles of music, which, by the end of the nineteenth century, produced a new artistic profession called "conducting."

One might ask how a conductor can "play" an orchestra when he or she is conducting only the rhythm? The strongest component of music, the rhythm is to the music what the skeleton is to the human form. If you take away the skeleton, you would no longer recognize the person. Aaron Copland, in his *Music and Imagination*[*], a series of lectures given at Harvard University in 1952, said, "What is the nature of this gift? First, a conception of rhythm not as mental exercise but as something basic to the body's rhythmic impulse." He also said on a different page, "This, the most primitive element in music, has always remained comparatively free of constraint. Rhythm was considered to

---

[*] *Music and Imagination*, (The Charles Eliot Norton Lectures), pg. 84 and pg. 71. ©1952

need no justification; it was judged by its naturalness of movement and limited by no laws other than those of unity and variety."

An event in my early life as a musician offers an illustration: At my graduation party from the Israeli Conservatory of Music in Jerusalem, several students prepared what were supposed to be amusing musical bits. On his turn, one young man walked to the stage, and before sitting at the piano announced to the students, faculty and guests, "I am going to play for you some themes from famous classical works. I will play them all in the soprano (top) line with the original harmonies—and the only change will be in the rhythm. As soon as you recognize the composition, shout out the title." He proceeded to play perhaps six compositions, including Schubert's famous second theme from his Unfinished Symphony, themes from Beethoven's Fifth and Ninth Symphonies, and concluded with a composition by a member of the faculty, who was present. At the end of each presentation there was a deadly, embarrassing silence. Not one of us—trained musicians—recognized any of the compositions, including the faculty member whose own composition was played! Rhythm was the skeleton that, when missing or altered, rendered the music unrecognizable.

By controlling the rhythm of a composition, by varying it here and there intentionally or intuitively, the conductor is playing the music and shaping it. There is a term in music called rubato. It was very popular in the late nineteenth century and beginning of the twentieth century. The performer, within a musical phrase, rushes part of the phrase, and then slows down another part of the phrase, or vice versa, stretches out the rhythm and then catches up toward the end of the phrase. Somehow that makes the music more expressive. Most musicians do that instinctively, and it is that instinct which gives uniqueness to the performance. Suzanne Bloch once quoted Pablo Picasso to me, "An artist's job is to draw a perfect circle. Since no human being can draw a perfect circle, there'll be some variations in every drawing of a perfect circle. Those variations will express the artist. However, if an artist starts concentrating on those variations to express himself, he loses the whole thing." In other words, the conductor should try to conduct the piece as he understands it perfectly, as if he were inside the head of the composer when it was written. He then internalizes it in his own head or heart. When he tries to perform it, since he is not a metronome and cannot achieve perfection, the variations will add humanity to the performance, and also the quality of greatness or mediocrity. The maestro, in his preparation, works on his skill, but the results of greatness appear as an amalgam, a multiplication of talent and skill.

Finally, I want to address the misconception that due to their place at the "head" of an ensemble, all conductors possess grandiose egos. In my relationships with dozens of conductors over the years, I have found that many of the greatest among them not only had a sense of humility but also were very, very generous. In the history of music there are many examples of great musicians who were generous to younger ones, and of those who gave credit to others who had helped them musically. I can recall two commonly cited examples: First, the great Renaissance composer Palestrina, who wrote in the introduction to a volume of motets by his student, Tomas Luis de Victoria, that he had learned a new expressive style from his student, and second, the more famous story of Robert Schuman announcing to the nineteenth-century world that the successor to Beethoven had arrived, and that his name was Johannes Brahms. I have found that the great, great majority of conductors I have worked with possessed these qualities of humility and generosity. Mark Lavri, in charge of the radio chorus in Israel, for example, preferred that I conduct his music, even though he, for all intents and purposes, seemed to have quite a sense of himself

and was quite capable of conducting. Likewise, my first teacher at the Israeli Conservatory in Jerusalem, Mr. Joseph Tal, who was director of the Conservatory and conductor of the Conservatory chorus, one day stopped a rehearsal, called my name and said, "From now on you are the conductor of the chorus and I will be your accompanist." I must admit that I did not think that this arrangement was going to work because I always expected my accompanists to follow my conducting and not the other way around. I did not expect *him*, the teacher, to follow *me*, the student, but that is exactly what he did, and I might add he was one of the best accompanists with whom I had the pleasure of working throughout my fifty-year career.

Abraham Kaplan conducting

– ABOUT THE AUTHOR –

Hailed by Leonard Bernstein as "a heaven-sent maestro," Abraham Kaplan is considered by many to be the greatest choral conductor of his generation and one of the most dynamic performers on the world stage. His contribution to the world of classical music includes numerous acclaimed choral and symphonic compositions, world premiere performances of well-known twentieth century pieces, and instruction of many of today's symphony and choral conductors. Over the years, Kaplan's own chorus, the Camerata Singers, have performed numerous times with the New York Philharmonic and other great orchestras around the world.

During his tenure as Director of Choral Studies at Juilliard School of Music during the 1960's and 1970's, Kaplan simultaneously held a teaching position at the School of Sacred Music of Union Theological Seminary and directed the choral program for the New York State Summer School of the Arts (1976-83), was Musical Director of the Collegiate Chorale in New York (1961-73), and music director of the Symphonic Choral Society of New York (1968-77). He later moved to Seattle, Washington, where he was Director of Choral Studies at the University of Washington (1977-2004), and Associate Conductor to Gerard Schwarz at the Seattle Symphony (1995-2000).

Kaplan's dynamic orchestra and choral guest conducting appearances include performances with the NBC Symphony, Israel Philharmonic, the Calgary Symphony Orchestra, the Little Symphony of St. Louis, the LENA Orchestra of New York, the Park East Orchestra, the Long Island Orchestra Da Camera, and the Kol Israel Orchestra. His musical sensitivity and mastery of chorus and orchestra deliver nothing short of "Choral Splendor" according to one New York Times critic. His own recorded compositions have been featured on CBS Television artistic programs, on regular broadcasts of the Crystal Cathedral's Hour of Power program, and on the award-winning Karl Haas Adventures in Music radio program, among others. His instrumental arrangements of other composers' works have been used pervasively in the industry, with over one hundred published pieces in regular circulation Dr. Robert Schuller, calling Kaplan "one of the great composers of the twentieth century," commissioned the maestro to write the inaugural body of music for the opening of the Crystal Cathedral in the early 1980s.

Today, Kaplan splits his time between Tel Aviv, London, New York, Los Angeles and Seattle, concentrating on his composition work, guest appearances and his family.

Camerata Singers at the White House. Standing in front, left to right: Mrs. Nixon, Urko Kekkonen (President of Finland), Abraham Kaplan, President R. M. Nixon.

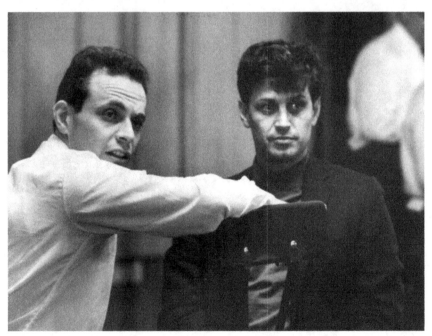

Lorin Maazel and Abraham Kaplan

Printed in the United States
By Bookmasters